MARK WOOD COLOR

ENGLAND CRICKETER

MR VIVEK KUMAR PANDEY SHAMBHUNATH

Disclaimer : During Writing This Book No character & No religious , No Relation Members Are Harmed. It's Only For Study & Entertainment Purpose. Do Not Take Seriously. Short Biopic Written In This Book Written By Mr Vivek Kumar Pandey.

Contents

Foreword

Short biography of Mark Wood and about life.During writing this book No character & No religious are harmed written by Mr Vivek Kumar Pandey. winner youngest writer award 1st rank in india 2020.He is only one writer can publish 870+ own book that was greatest successfull in his life.This All Credit Goes To My Super Hero Daddy. This book fully colour Edition.

Preface

Author biography in English :MY NAME IS VIVEK KUMAR PANDEY . I WAS BORN IN 30 SEP 2002,I AM FROM SURAT GUJARAT INDIA.MY DREAM WAS TO BE GOOD WRITERS ,MY FAMILY SUPPORTED ME TO SUCCESSFUL AND I CAN DO IT MY SELF.How do I write? That is a question, I believe, that can be honestly answered by me."CELEBRATING YOUNGEST WRITER AWARD WINNER IN GUJARAT 1ST RANK" MR PANDEY JI . I may think I did a good job writing something . The reader is the one who decides the quality of my writing. I do find writing to be natural to me and therefore find it to be a real challenge. My trick as a challenged writer is to do the best I can and know that I am happy with the final outcome. It may take a while to do my best and there may be quite a few problems I run into along the way.

I am not a greedy person those who are thinking about me and my self I never tried it anyone people suffering from sadness ,I trying to get promoted people suffering from happiness and joy in your Life Time. Now in current situation in India and also world people are unemployed and have no many but our indian governor help to people to get free food from ration card , i also take part in leadership team ,i am Motivational speaker , Film script writer. There was my two dream firstly writer and secondly actor & also my own film is upcoming soon i done almost completely completed script for my film .I AM GOING TO SAY WORD OF HEART TOUCH OUT PLEASE READ IT" , firstly i thanks my father he supports me in this field they always getting inspired me by own his words and behavior ,they always said that he was a biggest person in the world in future and also they purchase fruit and chocolate for me in anytime & anyway , firstly my father buy him then call me Vivek you want a chocolate i will say yes papa but how many tell me ,papa: you tell me how much i buy him i told 1 or 2 chocolate but my father purchase whole the boxes of chocolate and they get suprised me. MY FATHER WAS BORN IN " 20 SEPTEMBER" 1971 IN INDIA.

1) MY FATHER FAVORITE CLOTHES IS KURTA PAIJMA AND ALSO STYLES SHOE

2) FAVORITE SINGER IS KISHORE DA

3) FAVORITE STATE GUJARAT AND KOLKATA , HIS VILLAGE IN BIHAR

4) FAVORITE COLOR BLACK AND WHITE

THEY ALSO LOVE cricket like IPL and one day t-20 .they also like watching a News daily and heard the song daily ,they also interested in tik tok video but in current time tik tok is banned in india but also few videos are in you tube. In lockdown time my family and me very enjoy day daily. my father play daily ludo with his sister and son, daughter.they always loved tea and coffee anytime call me "। . I make it tea for my father but some reason after the April to june they are suffering from fever and cough , weakness on 6 June 2020 my father death. they not told me say bye bye his life. After death of 6 June on 10 june my mom and dad anniversary.but my father is Best in the world they can do anything for me please take care of father and respect it of your parents.

CHAPTER ONE

Mark Wood Color

- *Mark Wood Color*

1. Disclaimer : During Writing This Book No character & No religious , No Relation Members Are Harmed. It's Only For Study & Entertainment Purpose. Do Not Take Seriously. Short Biopic Written In This Book Written By Mr Vivek Kumar Pandey.

Mark Jason Wood (born 11 January 1990) is an English cricketer. Wood is a right-arm fast bowler who also bats right-handed. He represents England internationally in all forms of the game, and plays domestic cricket for Durham. Wood was part of the England squad that won the 2019 Cricket World Cup. Wood is currently one of the fastest bowlers in the world, having hit speeds up to 97mph (156kph).

- *Mark Wood Domestic career*

Wood made his debut in county cricket for Northumberland in 2008 against Norfolk in the MCCA Knockout Trophy. He played Minor counties cricket for Northumberland from 2008 to 2010, making 3 Minor Counties Championship appearances and 3 MCCA Knockout Trophy appearances.

- *Durham*

In the 2011 season, he made his debut for Durham in a first-class match against Durham MCCU. He followed this up by making his List A debut against Northamptonshire in the 2011 Clydesdale Bank 40.He has since made a further first-class appearance against Sri Lanka A, and a further List

A appearance against Scotland in the Clydesdale Bank 40.Wood made his debut for the England Lions in their 2014 tour of Sri Lanka.

- *Indian Premier League*

On 28 January 2018, Wood was bought by Chennai Super Kings for INR 1.5 crores (£160,000) for the 2018 IPL season.

- *Mark Wood International career*

2015: West Indies and Ireland

In March 2015, Wood was named in the England Test squad for the tour of the West Indies. However, he did not play in the series.He made his One-Day International debut for England against Ireland on 8 May 2015. The match was affected by rain and little cricket was played, although Wood did take his first international wicket.

- *Mark Wood in 2015: New Zealand*

He made his Test debut for England later the same month against New Zealand. In the first Test Wood took figures of 3–93 in New Zealand's first innings. He then took 1–47 in their second innings to help England win the match by 124 runs and go 1-0 up in the series. In the following Test Wood continued to impress, taking figures of 2–62 in New Zealand's first innings. He also made a useful 19 with the bat. In New Zealand's second innings he took another three wickets, this time at the expense of 97 runs. England lost the match by 199 runs and the series was drawn at 1-1.

Wood played in the third ODI against New Zealand, taking figures of 1-48. In the next game he took figure of 1–49 to help England win by seven wickets and level the series at 2-2. Although Wood did not take a wicket in the final game of the series, taking 0-70, England still won to win the series 3–1.

He made his Twenty20 International debut in the same series on 23 June 2015. He finished with figures of 3-26 as England won by 56 runs.

- *Mark Wood 2015: Ashes series*

Wood taking the final wicket of the Fourth Test of the 2015 Ashes series at Trent Bridge

Wood took 2–68 in Australia's first innings of the first Ashes Test and followed this up by taking 2–53 in their second innings to help England win the match by 169 runs. In the second Test he only took one wicket in the Australian first innings, finishing with figures of 1-92 as England lost the match by 405 runs. He was ruled out of the third Test through injury, but returned in the fourth Test, taking 1–13 in Australia's first innings. In the second innings he took figures of 3-69 including the wicket that won the match for England, which meant they regained the Ashes. England lost the final Test of the series, with Wood taking 1–59 in Australia first innings. However, England won the series 3–2 to regain the Ashes.

Wood was selected for the first ODI against Australia, although he was expensive, finishing with figures of 1-72 as Australia won the game. He kept his place for the next game, but he again proved expensive, this time finishing with 0-65 from his nine overs, although England went on to win the game by three wickets. After being dropped from the side for the next two games, he returned for the final ODI and took figures of 1-25, although a poor batting performance from England meant they lost the game and the series 3–2.

- *Mark Wood in 2015: Pakistan*

He played in the first Test against Pakistan although he only picked up one wicket in the match, which ended in a draw, as England were unable to force a win due to bad light. He played in the second Test, which England lost, although he performed well. He took 3–39 in Pakistan's first innings and followed this up with another two wickets in the second innings, although Pakistan went on to win the match in convincing fashion, by 178 runs.

An ankle injury ruled Wood out of England's entire series against Sri Lanka, and he also missed the start of the return series against Pakistan.

- *Mark Wood in 2016: Pakistan*

Wood returned from injury in time for the first ODI against Pakistan. He took figures of 1-57 as England won by 44 runs on the D/L Method. He took 3/46 in the next match as England restricted Pakistan to 251 and won the match by four wickets. In the third match of the series he took figures of 1-75 as England won by 169 runs. After missing the fourth match, he returned for the final match of the series and took figures of 2-56, although England lost the match by four wickets, although they won the series 4–1.

- *Mark Wood in 2019: West Indies*

Wood was called up to replace injured Olly Stone in a 3-test tour of the West Indies. He did not play in the first 2 matches, both of which England lost, but was drafted in to the team for the third test in St.Lucia. Wood bowled the fastest of any bowler in the match and in the Windies' first innings took 5 wickets for 41 runs off 8.2 overs - his first five-wicket Test haul helping England to a 142-run lead over West Indies on day two of the final test.

- *Mark Wood 2019 Cricket World Cup*

In April 2019, he was named in England's squad for the 2019 Cricket World Cup. On 14 June 2019, in the match against the West Indies, Wood took his 50th wicket in ODIs. On 11 July 2019, in the semi-final against Australia, Wood played in his 50th ODI match for England. In the Cricket World Cup Final, Wood, batting at number 11, was run out off the last ball of the match which led to the game going to a Super Over.Wood also sustained a side injury during the game, which ruled him out of the first three Tests of the 2019 Ashes series.

- *Mark Wood in 2020 and 2021*

After missing the 2019 Ashes series and tour of New Zealand, Wood returned to Test cricket in the third test of the 2019-20 tour of South Africa following injuries to James Anderson and Jofra Archer. After scoring 42 runs from 23 balls in England's first innings, he took 3/32 in South Africa's second innings as England won. In the fourth test, Wood took nine wickets, including 5/46 in South Africa's first innings, and scored 35 with the bat as England won again.

On 29 May 2020, Wood was named in a 55-man group of players to begin training ahead of international fixtures starting in England following the COVID-19 pandemic. On 17 June 2020, Wood was included in England's 30-man squad to start training behind closed doors for the Test series against the West Indies. On 4 July 2020, Wood was named in England's thirteen-man squad for the first Test match of the series.

In September 2021, Wood was named in England's squad for the 2021 ICC Men's T20 World Cup.

Wood was selected for the 2021–22 Ashes.

CHAPTER TWO

England Cricket Team

- England Cricket Team

1. Disclaimer : During Writing This Book No character & No religious , No Relation Members Are Harmed. It's Only For Study & Entertainment Purpose. Do Not Take Seriously. Short Biopic Written In This Book Written By Mr Vivek Kumar Pandey.

The England cricket team represents England and Wales in international cricket. Since 1997, it has been governed by the England and Wales Cricket Board (ECB), having been previously governed by Marylebone Cricket Club (the MCC) since 1903. England, as a founding nation, is a Full Member of the International Cricket Council (ICC) with Test, One Day International (ODI) and Twenty20 International (T20I) status. Until the 1990s, Scottish and Irish players also played for England as those countries were not yet ICC members in their own right.

England and Australia were the first teams to play a Test match (15–19 March 1877), and along with South Africa, these nations formed the Imperial Cricket Conference (the predecessor to today's International Cricket Council) on 15 June 1909. England and Australia also played the first ODI on 5 January 1971. England's first T20I was played on 13 June 2005, once more against Australia.

As of December 2021, England have played 1,044 Test matches, winning 378 and losing 314 (with 352 draws). In Test series against Australia, England play for The Ashes, one of the most famous trophies in all of sport, and they have won the urn on 32 occasions. England have also played 760 ODIs, winning 383. They have appeared in the final of the Cricket World Cup four times, winning once in 2019; they have also finished as runners-up in two ICC Champions Trophies (2004 and 2013). England have played 143 T20Is, winning 75.They won the ICC T20 World Cup in 2010, and were runners-up in 2016.As of 12 November 2021, England are ranked fourth in Tests, second in ODIs and first in T20Is by the ICC.

- The All-England Eleven in 1846

The first recorded incidence of a team with a claim to represent England comes from 9 July 1739 when an "All-England" team, which consisted of 11 gentlemen from any part of England exclusive of Kent, played against "the Unconquerable County" of Kent and lost by a margin of "very few notches". Such matches were repeated on numerous occasions for the best part of a century.

In 1846 William Clarke formed the All-England Eleven. This team eventually competed against a United All-England Eleven with annual matches occurring between 1847 and 1856. These matches were arguably the most important contest of the English season if judged by the quality of the players.

- Early tours

The first overseas tour occurred in September 1859 with England touring North America. This team had six players from the All-England Eleven, six from the United All-England Eleven and was captained by George Parr.

With the outbreak of the American Civil War, attention turned elsewhere. English tourists visited Australia in 1861–62 with this first tour organised as a commercial venture by Messrs Spiers and Pond, restaurateurs of Melbourne. Most matches played during tours prior to 1877 were "against odds", with the opposing team fielding more than 11 players to make for a more even contest. This first Australian tour were mostly against odds of at least 18/11.

- The first England team to tour southern Australia in 1861–62

The tour was so successful that Parr led a second tour in 1863–64. James Lillywhite led a subsequent England team which sailed on the P&O steamship Poonah on 21 September 1876. They played a combined

Australian XI, for once on even terms of 11-a-side. The match, starting on 15 March 1877 at the Melbourne Cricket Ground came to be regarded as the inaugural Test match. The combined Australian XI won this Test match by 45 runs with Charles Bannerman of Australia scoring the first Test century. At the time, the match was promoted as James Lillywhite's XI v Combined Victoria and New South Wales. The teams played a return match on the same ground at Easter, 1877, when Lillywhite's team avenged their loss with a victory by four wickets. The first Test match on English soil occurred in 1880 with England victorious; this was the first time England fielded a fully representative side with W. G. Grace included in the team.

- 1880s

As a result of this loss, the tour of 1882–83 was dubbed by England captain Ivo Bligh as "the quest to regain the ashes". England, with a mixture of amateurs and professionals, won the series 2–1. Bligh was presented with an urn that contained some ashes, which have variously been said to be of a bail, ball or even a woman's veil, and so The Ashes was born. A fourth match was then played which Australia won by four wickets. However, the match was not considered part of the Ashes series. England dominated many of these early contests with England winning the Ashes series 10 times between 1884 and 1898. During this period England also played their first Test match against South Africa in 1889 at Port Elizabeth.

- 1890s

England won the 1890 Ashes series 2–0, with the third match of the series being the first Test match to be abandoned. England lost 2–1 in the 1891–92 series, although England regained the urn the following year. England again won the 1894–95 series, winning 3–2 under the leadership of Andrew Stoddart. In 1895–96, England played South Africa, winning all Tests in the series. The 1899 Ashes series was the first tour where the MCC and the counties appointed a selection committee. There were three active players: Grace, Lord Hawke and Warwickshire captain Herbert Bainbridge. Prior to this, England teams for home Tests had been chosen by the club on whose ground the match was to be played. England lost the 1899 Ashes series 1–0, with Grace making his final Test appearance in the first match of the series.

- 1900s

The start of the 20th century saw mixed results for England as they lost four of the eight Ashes series between 1900 and 1914. During this period, England lost their first series against South Africa in the 1905–06 season 4–1 as their batting faltered.

England lost their first series of the new century to Australia in 1901–02 Ashes. Australia also won the 1902 series, which was memorable for exciting cricket, including Gilbert Jessop scoring a Test century in just 70 minutes. England regained the Ashes in 1904 under the captaincy of Pelham Warner. R. E. Foster scored 287 on his debut and Wilfred Rhodes took 15 wickets in a match. In 1905–06, England lost 4–1 against South Africa. England avenged the defeat in 1907, when they won the series 1–0 under the captaincy of Foster. However, they lost the 1909 Ashes series against Australia, suing 25 players in the process. England also lost to South Africa, with Jack Hobbs scoring his first of 15 centuries on the tour.

- 1910s

England toured Australia in 1911–12 and beat their opponents 4–1. The team included the likes of Rhodes, Hobbs, Frank Woolley and Sydney Barnes. England lost the first match of the series but bounced back and won the next four Tests. This proved to be the last Ashes series before the war.

The 1912 season saw England take part in a unique experiment. A nine-Test triangular tournament involving England, South Africa and Australia was set up. The series was hampered by a very wet summer and player disputes however and the tournament was considered a failure with the Daily Telegraph stating:

Nine Tests provide a surfeit of cricket, and contests between Australia and South Africa are not a great attraction to the British public.With Australia sending a weakened team and the South African bowlers being ineffective England dominated the tournament winning four of their six matches. The match between Australia and South Africa at Lord's was visited by King George V, the first time a reigning monarch had watched Test cricket. England went on one more tour before the outbreak of the First World War, beating South Africa 4–0, with Barnes taking 49 wickets in the series.

- 1920s

England's first match after the war was in the 1920–21 season against Australia. Still feeling the effects of the war England went down to a series of crushing defeats and suffered their first whitewash losing the series 5–0. Six Australians scored hundreds while Mailey spun out 36 English batsmen. Things were no better in the next few Ashes series losing the 1921 Ashes series 3–0 and the 1924–25 Ashes 4–1. England's fortunes were to change in 1926 as they regained the Ashes and were a formidable team during this period dispatching Australia 4–1 in the 1928–29 Ashes tour.

On the same year the West Indies became the fourth nation to be granted Test status and played their first game against England. England won each of these three Tests by an innings, and a view was expressed in the press that their elevation had proved a mistake although Learie Constantine did the double on the tour. In the 1929–30 season England went on two concurrent tours with one team going to New Zealand (who were granted Test status earlier that year) and the other to the West Indies. Despite sending two separate teams England won both tours beating New Zealand 1–0 and the West Indies 2–1.

- 1930s

The 1930 Ashes series saw a young Don Bradman dominate the tour, scoring 974 runs in his seven Test innings. He scored 254 at Lord's, 334 at Headingley and 232 at The Oval. Australia regained the Ashes winning the series 3–1. As a result of Bradman's prolific run-scoring the England captain Douglas Jardine chose to develop the already existing leg theory into fast leg theory, or bodyline, as a tactic to stop Bradman. Fast leg theory involved bowling fast balls directly at the batsman's body. The batsman would need to defend himself, and if he touched the ball with the bat, he risked being caught by one of a large number of fielders placed on the leg side.

English cricket team at the Test match held at the Brisbane Exhibition Ground. England won the match by a record margin of 675 runs.Using Jardine's fast leg theory, England won the next Ashes series 4–1, but complaints about the Bodyline tactic caused crowd disruption on the tour, and threats of diplomatic action from the Australian Cricket Board, which during the tour sent the following cable to the MCC in London:

Bodyline bowling assumed such proportions as to menace best interests of game, making protection of body by batsmen the main consideration. Causing intensely bitter feeling between players as well as injury. In our opinion is unsportsmanlike. Unless stopped at once likely to upset friendly relations existing between Australia and England.

Later, Jardine was removed from the captaincy and the Laws of Cricket changed so that no more than one fast ball aimed at the body was permitted per over, and having more than two fielders behind square leg was banned.

England's following tour of India in the 1933–34 season was the first Test match to be staged in the subcontinent. The series was also notable for Stan Nichols and Nobby Clark bowling so many bouncers that the Indian batsman wore solar toupées instead of caps to protect themselves.

Australia won the 1934 Ashes series 2–1 and kept the urn for the following 19 years. Many of the wickets of the time were friendly to batsmen resulting in a large proportion of matches ending in high scoring draws and many batting records being set.

England drew the 1938 Ashes, meaning Australia retained the urn. England went into the final match of the series at The Oval 1–0 down, but won the final game by an innings and 579 runs. Len Hutton made the highest ever Test score by an Englishman, making 364 in England first innings to help them reach 903, their highest ever score against Australia.

The 1938–39 tour of South Africa saw another experiment with the deciding Test being a timeless Test that was played to a finish. England lead 1–0 going into the final timeless match at Durban. Despite the final Test being 'timeless', the game ended in a draw after 10 days as England had to catch the train to catch the boat home. A record 1,981 runs were scored, and the concept of timeless Tests was abandoned. England went on one final tour of the West Indies in 1939 before the Second World War, although a team for an MCC tour of India was selected more in hope than expectation of the matches being played.

- 1940s

Test cricket resumed after the war in 1946, and England won their first match back against India. However, they struggled in the 1946–47 Ashes series, losing 3–0 in Australia under Wally Hammond's captaincy. England beat South Africa 3–0 in 1947 with Denis Compton scoring 1,187 runs in the series.

The 1947–48 series against the West Indies was another disappointment for England, with the side losing 2–0 following injuries to several key players. England suffered further humiliation against Bradman's invincible side in the 1948 Ashes series. Hutton was controversially dropped for the third Test, and England were bowled out for just 52 at The Oval. The series proved to be Bradman's final Ashes series.

In 1948–49, England beat South Africa 2–0 under the captaincy of George Mann. The series included a record breaking stand of 359 between Hutton and Cyril Washbrook. The decade ended with England drawing the Test series against New Zealand, with every match ending in a draw.

- 1950s

Their fortunes changed on the 1953 Ashes tour as they won the series 1–0. England did not lose a series between their 1950–51 and 1958–59 tours of Australia and secured famous victory in 1954–55 under the captaincy of Len Hutton, thanks to Frank Tyson whose 6/85 at Sydney and 7/27 at Melbourne are remembered as the fastest bowling ever seen in Australia. The 1956 series was remembered for the bowling of Jim Laker who took 46 wickets at an average of 9.62, including figures of 19/90 at Old Trafford. After drawing to South Africa, England defeated the West Indies and New Zealand comfortably.

The England team then left for Australia in the 1958–59 season with a team that had been hailed as the strongest ever to leave on an Ashes tour but lost the series 4–0 as Richie Benaud's revitalised Australians were too strong, with England struggling with the bat throughout the series.

On 24 August 1959, England inflicted its only 5–0 whitewash over India. All out for 194 at The Oval, India lost the last test by an innings. England's batsman Ken Barrington and Colin Cowdrey both had an excellent series with the bat, with Barrington scoring 357 runs across the series and Cowdrey scoring 344.

- 1960s

The early and middle 1960s were poor periods for English cricket. Despite England's strength on paper, Australia held the Ashes and the West Indies dominated England in the early part of the decade. May stood down as captain in 1961 following the 1961 Ashes defeat.

Ted Dexter succeeded him as captain but England continued to suffer indifferent results. In 1961–62, they beat Pakistan, but also lost to India. The following year saw England and Australia tie the 1962–63 Ashes series 1–1, meaning Australia retained the urn. Despite beating New Zealand 3–0, England went on to lose to the West Indies, and again failed in the 1964 Ashes, losing the home series 1–0, which marked the end of Dexter's captaincy.

However, from 1968 to 1971 they played 27 consecutive Test matches without defeat, winning 9 and drawing 18 (including the abandoned Test at Melbourne in 1970–71). The sequence began when they drew with Australia at Lord's in the Second Test of the 1968 Ashes series and ended in 1971 when India won the Third Test at The Oval by four wickets. They played 13 Tests with only one defeat immediately beforehand and so played a total of 40 consecutive Tests with only one defeat, dating from their innings victory over the West Indies at The Oval in 1966. During this period they beat New Zealand, India, the West Indies, and Pakistan, and under Ray Illingworth's leadership, regained The Ashes from Australia in 1970–71.

- 1970s

The 1970s, for the England team, can be largely split into three parts. Early in the decade, Illingworth's side dominated world cricket, winning the Ashes away in 1971 and then retaining them at home in 1972. The same side beat Pakistan at home in 1971 and played by far the better cricket against India that season. However, England were largely helped by the rain to sneak the Pakistan series 1–0 but the same rain saved India twice and one England collapse saw them lose to India. This was, however, one of (if not the) strongest England team ever with the likes of Illingworth, Geoffrey Boycott, John Edrich, Basil D'Oliveira, Dennis Amiss, Alan Knott, John Snow and Derek Underwood at its core.

The mid-1970s were more turbulent. Illingworth and several others had refused to tour India in 1972–73 which led to a clamour for Illingworth's job by the end of that summer – England had just been beaten 2–0 by a flamboyant West Indies side – with several England players well over 35. Mike Denness was the surprising choice but only lasted 18 months; his results against poor opposition were good, but England were badly exposed as ageing and lacking in good fast bowling against the 1974–75 Australians, losing that series 4–1 to lose the Ashes.

Denness was replaced in 1975 by Tony Greig. While he managed to avoid losing to Australia, his side were largely thrashed the following year by the young and very much upcoming West Indies for whom Greig's infamous "grovel" remark acted as motivation. Greig's finest hour was probably the 1976–77 win over India in India. When Greig was discovered as being instrumental in World Series Cricket, he was sacked, and replaced by Mike Brearley.

Brearley's side showed again the hyperbole that is often spoken when one side dominates in cricket. While his side of 1977–80 contained some young players who went on to become England greats, most notably future captains Ian Botham, David Gower and Graham Gooch, their opponents were often very much weakened by the absence of their World Series players, especially in 1978, when England beat New Zealand 3–0 and Pakistan 2–0 before thrashing what was effectively Australia's 2nd XI 5–1 in 1978–79.

- 1980s

The England team, with Brearley's exit in 1980, was never truly settled throughout the 1980s, which will probably be remembered as a low point for the team. While some of the great players like Botham, Gooch and Gower had fine careers, the team seldom succeeded in beating good opposition throughout the decade and did not score a home Test victory between September 1985 and July 1990.

Botham took over the captaincy in 1980 and they put up a good fight against the West Indies, losing a five match Test series 1–0, although England were humbled in the return series. After scoring a pair in the first Test against Australia, Botham lost the captaincy due to his poor form, and was replaced by Brearley. Botham returned to form and played exceptionally in the remainder of the series, being named man of the match in the third, fourth and fifth Tests. The series became known as Botham's Ashes as England recorded a 3–1 victory.

Keith Fletcher took over as captain in 1981, but England lost his first series in charge against India. Bob Willis took over as captain in 1982 and enjoyed victories over India and Pakistan, but lost the Ashes after Australia clinched the series 2–1. England hosted the World Cup in 1983 and reached the semi-finals, but their Test form remained poor, as they suffered defeats against New Zealand, Pakistan and the West Indies.

Gower took over as skipper in 1984 and led the team to a 2–1 victory over India. They went on to win the 1985 Ashes 3–1, although after this came a poor run of form. Defeat to the West Indies dented the team's confidence, and they went on to lose to India 2–0. In 1986, Micky Stewart was appointed the first full-time England coach. England beat New Zealand, but there was little hope of them retaining the Ashes in 1986–87. However, despite being described as a team that 'can't bat, can't bowl and can't field', they went on to win the series 2–1.

After losing consecutive series against Pakistan, England drew a three match Test series against New Zealand 0–0. They reached the final of the 1987 World Cup, but lost by seven runs against Australia. After losing 4–0 to the West Indies, England lost the Ashes to a resurgent Australia led by Allan Border. With the likes of Gooch banned following a rebel tour to South Africa, a new look England side suffered defeat again against the West Indies, although this time by a margin of 2–1.

- 1990s

If the 1980s were a low point for English Test cricket, then the 1990s were only a slight improvement. The arrival of Gooch as captain in 1990 forced a move toward more professionalism and especially fitness though it took some time for old habits to die. Even in 2011, one or two successful county players have been shown up as physically unfit for international cricket. Creditable performances against India and New Zealand in 1990 were followed by a hard-fought draw against the 1991 West Indies and a strong performance in the 1992 Cricket World Cup in which the England team finished as runners-up for the second consecutive World Cup, but landmark losses against Australia in 1990–91 and especially Pakistan in 1992 showed England up badly in terms of bowling. So bad was England's bowling in 1993 that Rod Marsh described England's pace attack at one point as "pie throwers". Having lost three of the first four Tests played in England in 1993, Gooch resigned to be replaced by Michael Atherton.

More selectorial problems abounded during Atherton's reign as new chairman of selectors and coach Ray Illingworth (then into his 60s) assumed almost sole responsibility for the team off the field. The youth policy which had seen England emerge from the West Indies tour of 1993–94 with some credit (though losing to a seasoned Windies team) was abandoned and players such as Gatting and Gooch were persisted with when well into their 30s and 40s. England continued to do well at home against weaker opponents such as India, New Zealand and a West Indies side beginning to fade but struggled badly against improving sides like Pakistan and South Africa.

Atherton had offered his resignation after losing the 1997 Ashes series 3–2 having been 1–0 up after two matches – eventually to resign one series later in early 1998. England, looking for talent, went through a whole raft of new players during this period, such as Ronnie Irani, Adam Hollioake, Craig White, Graeme Hick and Mark Ramprakash. At this time, there were two main problems:The lack of a genuine all-rounder to bat at 6, Botham having left a huge gap in the batting order when he retired from Tests in 1992.

Alec Stewart, a sound wicket-keeper and an excellent player of quick bowling, could not open and keep wicket, hence his batting down the order, where he was often exposed to spin which he did not play as well.

Stewart took the reins as captain in 1998, but another losing Ashes series and early World Cup exit cost him Test and ODI captaincy in 1999. This should not detract from the 1998 home Test series where England showed great fortitude to beat a powerful South African side 2–1.

Another reason for their poor performances were the demands of County Cricket teams on their players, meaning that England could rarely field a full-strength team on their tours. This eventually led to the ECB taking over from the MCC as the governing body of England and the implementation of central contracts. 1992 also saw Scotland sever ties with the England and Wales team, and begin to compete as the Scotland national team.

By 1999, with coach David Lloyd resigning after the World Cup exit and new captain Nasser Hussain just appointed, England hit rock bottom after losing 2–1 to New Zealand in shambolic fashion. Hussain was booed on the Oval balcony as the crowd jeered "We’ve got the worst team in the world" to the tune of "He’s Got the Whole World in His Hands".

- 2000s

Central contracts were installed – reducing players workloads – and following the arrival of Zimbabwean coach Duncan Fletcher, England thrashed the fallen West Indies 3–1. England’s results in Asia improved that winter with series wins against both Pakistan and Sri Lanka. Hussain’s side had a far harder edge to it, avoiding the anticipated "Greenwash" in the 2001

Ashes series against the all-powerful Australian team. The nucleus the side was slowly coming together as players such as Hussain himself, Graham Thorpe, Darren Gough and Ashley Giles began to be regularly selected. By 2003 though, having endured another Ashes drubbing as well as another first-round exit from the World Cup, Hussain resigned as captain after one Test against South Africa.

Michael Vaughan took over, with players encouraged to express themselves. England won five consecutive Test series prior to facing Australia in the 2005 Ashes series, taking the team to second place in the ICC Test Championship table. During this period England defeated the West Indies home and away, New Zealand, and Bangladesh at home, and South Africa in South Africa. In June 2005, England played its first ever T20 international match, defeating Australia by 100 runs. Later that year, England defeated Australia 2–1 in a thrilling series to regain the Ashes for the first time in 16 years, having lost them in 1989. Following the 2005 Ashes win, the team suffered from a spate of serious injuries to key players such as Vaughan, Giles, Andrew Flintoff and Simon Jones. As a result, the team underwent an enforced period of transition. A 2–0 defeat in Pakistan was followed by two drawn away series with India and Sri Lanka.

In the home Test series victory against Pakistan in July and August 2006, several promising new players emerged. Most notable were the left-arm orthodox spin bowler Monty Panesar, the first Sikh to play Test cricket for England, and left-handed opening batsman Alastair Cook. The 2006–07 Ashes series was keenly anticipated and was expected to provide a level of competition comparable to the 2005 series. In the event, England, captained by Flintoff who was deputising for the injured Vaughan, lost all five Tests to concede the first Ashes whitewash in 86 years.

In the 2007 Cricket World Cup, England lost to most of the Test playing nations they faced, beating only the West Indies and Bangladesh, although they also avoided defeat by any of the non-Test playing nations. Even so, the unimpressive nature of most of their victories in the tournament, combined with heavy defeats by New Zealand, Australia and South Africa, left many commentators criticising the manner in which the England team approached the one-day game. Coach Duncan Fletcher resigned after eight years in the job as a result and was succeeded by former Sussex coach Peter Moores.

In 2007–08, England toured Sri Lanka and New Zealand, losing the first series 1–0 and winning the second 2–1. These series were followed up at home in May 2008 with a 2–0 home series win against New Zealand, with the results easing pressure on Moores – who was not at ease with his team, particularly star batsman Kevin Pietersen. Pietersen succeeded Vaughan as captain in June 2008, after England had been well beaten by South Africa at home. The poor relationship between the two came to a head on the 2008–09 tour to India. England lost the series 1–0 and both men resigned their positions, although Pietersen remained a member of the England team. Moores was replaced as coach by Zimbabwean Andy Flower. Against this background, England toured the West Indies under the captaincy of Andrew Strauss and, in a disappointing performance, lost the Test series 1–0.

The 2009 Ashes series featured the first Test match played in Wales, at Sophia Gardens, Cardiff. England drew the match thanks to a last-wicket stand by bowlers James Anderson and Panesar. A victory for each team followed before the series was decided at The Oval. Thanks to fine bowling by Stuart Broad and Graeme Swann and a debut century by Jonathan Trott, England regained the Ashes.

- 2010s

After a drawn Test series in South Africa, England won their first ever ICC world championship, the 2010 World Twenty20, with a seven-wicket win over Australia in Barbados. The following winter in the 2010–11 Ashes, they beat Australia 3–1 to retain the urn and record their first series win in Australia for 24 years. Furthermore, all three of their wins were by an innings – the first time a touring side had ever recorded three innings victories in a single Test series. Cook earned Man of the Series with 766 runs.

England struggled to match their Test form in the 2011 Cricket World Cup. Despite beating South Africa and tying with eventual winners India, England suffered shock losses to Ireland and Bangladesh before losing in the quarter-finals to Sri Lanka.However the team's excellent form in the Test match arena continued and on 13 August 2011, they became the world's top-ranked Test team after comfortably whitewashing India 4–0, their sixth consecutive series victory and eighth in the past nine series. However, this status only lasted a year – having lost 3–0 to Pakistan over the winter, England were beaten 2–0 by South Africa, who replaced them at the top of the rankings. It was their first home series loss since 2008, against the same opposition.

This loss saw the resignation of Strauss as captain (and his retirement from cricket). Cook, who was already in charge of the ODI side, replaced Strauss and led England to a 2–1 victory in India – their first in the country since 1984–85. In doing so, he became the first captain to score centuries in his first five Tests as captain and became England's leading century-maker with 23 centuries to his name.

- The England team celebrate victory over Australia in the 2015 Ashes series

After finishing as runners-up in the ICC Champions Trophy, England faced Australia in back-to-back Ashes series. A 3–0 home win secured England the urn for the fourth time in five series. However, in the return series, they found themselves utterly demolished in a 5–0 defeat, their second Ashes whitewash in under a decade. Their misery was compounded by batsman Jonathan Trott leaving the tour early due to a stress-related illness and the mid-series retirement of spinner Graeme Swann. Following the tour, head coach Flower resigned his post while Pietersen was dropped indefinitely from the England team.

Flower was replaced by his predecessor, Moores, but he was sacked for a second time after a string of disappointing results including failing to advance from the group stage at the 2015 World Cup. He was replaced by Australian Trevor Bayliss who oversaw an upturn of form in the ODI side, including series victories against New Zealand and Pakistan. In the Test arena, England reclaimed the Ashes 3–2 in the summer of 2015.

England entered the 2019 Cricket World Cup as favourites, having been ranked the number one ODI side by the ICC for over a year prior to the tournament. However, shock defeats to Pakistan and Sri Lanka during the group stage left them on the brink of elimination and needing to win their final two games against India and New Zealand to guarantee progression to the semi-finals. This was achieved, putting their campaign back on track, and an eight-wicket victory over Australia in the semi-final at Edgbaston meant England were in their first World Cup final since 1992. The final against New Zealand at Lord's has been described as one of the greatest and most dramatic matches in the history of cricket, with some calling it the "greatest ODI in history", as both the match and subsequent Super Over were tied, after England went into the final over of their innings 14 runs behind New Zealand's total. England won by virtue of having scored more boundaries throughout the match, securing their maiden World Cup title in their fourth final appearance.

- England and Wales Cricket Board

The England and Wales Cricket Board (ECB) is the governing body of English cricket and the England cricket team. The Board has been operating since 1 January 1997 and represents England on the International Cricket Council. The ECB is also responsible for the generation of income from the sale of tickets, sponsorship and broadcasting rights, primarily in relation to the England team. The ECB's income in the 2006 calendar year was £77 million.

Prior to 1997, the Test and County Cricket Board (TCCB) was the governing body for the English team. Apart from in Test matches, when touring abroad, the England team officially played as MCC up to and including the 1976–77 tour of Australia, reflecting the time when MCC had been responsible for selecting the touring party. The last time the England touring team wore the bacon-and-egg colours of the MCC was on the 1996–97 tour of New Zealand.

- Status of Wales

Historically, the England team represented the whole of Great Britain in international cricket, with Scottish or Welsh national teams playing sporadically and players from both countries occasionally representing England. Scotland became an independent member of the ICC in 1994, having severed links with the TCCB two years earlier.

Criticism has been made of the England and Wales Cricket Board using only the England name while utilising Welsh players such as Simon and Geraint Jones. With Welsh players pursuing international careers exclusively with an England team, there have been a number of calls for Wales to become an independent member of the ICC, or for the ECB to provide more fixtures for a Welsh national team.However, both Cricket Wales and Glamorgan County Cricket Club have continually supported the ECB, with Glamorgan arguing for the financial benefits of the Welsh county within the English structure, and Cricket Wales stating they are "committed to continuing to play a major role within the ECB".

The absence of a Welsh cricket team has seen a number of debates within the Welsh Senedd. In 2013 a debate saw both Conservative and Labour members lend their support to the establishment of an independent Welsh team.

In 2015, a report produced by the Welsh National Assembly's petitions committee, reflected the passionate debate around the issue. Bethan Jenkins, Plaid Cymru's spokesperson on heritage, culture, sport and broadcasting, and a member of the petitions committee, argued that Wales should have its own international team and withdraw from the ECB. Jenkins noted that Ireland (with a population of 6.4 million) was an ICC member with 6,000 club players whereas Wales (with 3 million) had 7,500. Jenkins said: "Cricket Wales and Glamorgan CCC say the idea of a Welsh national cricket team is 'an emotive subject', of course having a national team is emotive, you only have to look at the stands during any national game to see that. To suggest this as anything other than natural is a bit of a misleading argument."

In 2017, the First Minister of Wales, Carwyn Jones called for the reintroduction of the Welsh one-day team stating: "[It] is odd that we see Ireland and Scotland playing in international tournaments and not Wales."

- England at 2021

In February 2021, England and Wales Cricket Board announced that England's Principal partner NatWest has been replaced by Cinch, an online used car marketplace. England's kit is manufactured by New Balance, who replaced previous manufacturer Adidas in April 2017.

When playing Test cricket, England's cricket whites feature the three lions badge on the left of the shirt and the name of the sponsor Cinch on the centre. English fielders may wear a navy blue cap or white sun hat with the ECB logo in the middle. Helmets are also coloured navy blue. Before 1997 the uniform sported the TCCB lion and stumps logo on the uniforms, while the helmets, jumpers and hats had the three lions emblem.

In limited overs cricket, England's ODI and Twenty20 shirts feature the Cinch logo across the centre, with the three lions badge on the left of the shirt and the New Balance logo on the right. In ODIs, the kit comprises a blue shirt with navy trousers, whilst the Twenty20 kit comprises a flame red shirt and navy trousers. In ICC limited-overs tournaments, a modified kit design is used with sponsor's logo moving to the sleeve and 'ENGLAND' printed across the front.

Over the years, England's ODI kit has cycled between various shades of blue (such as a pale blue used until the mid-1990s, when it was replaced in favour of a bright blue) with the occasional all-red kit.In April 2017, ECB brought back traditional cable-knit sweater for test matches under new supplier New Balance.

CHAPTER THREE

History of the England cricket

• History of the England cricket

The history of the England cricket team can be said to date back to at least 1739, when sides styled "Kent" and "All England" played a match at Bromley Common. Over 300 matches involving "England" or "All England" prior to 1877 are known. However these teams were usually put together on an ad hoc basis and were rarely fully representative.

The history of the current England side can be traced to 1877 when England played in what was subsequently recognised as the very first Test match. Since then, up to 20 August 2006 they have played 852 Test matches, winning 298, losing 245 and drawing 309. During these 852 matches, they have been captained by 77 different players.

• Early history

The term "All-England" was first used in reports of two Kent v All-England matches in July 1739.

The first match was at Bromley Common in Kent on Monday 9 July 1739. It was billed as between "eleven gentlemen of that county (i.e., Kent) and eleven gentlemen from any part of England, exclusive of Kent". Kent, described as "the Unconquerable County" won by "a very few notches".

The second match was at the Artillery Ground in Bunhill Fields, Finsbury on Monday 23 July 1739. This game was drawn and a report includes the phrase "eleven picked out of all England".

In subsequent decades there were many more such matches between a side representing a county, or the MCC, and a side drawn from the rest of England and described as "England" or "All England". As the next section describes, in 1846 the term "All England Eleven" would acquire a new, more precise, definition.

- The All-England XI

In 1846 William Clarke formed the All-England Eleven as a touring team of leading players to play matches at big city venues, mainly in the North of England. Clarke's team was a top-class side worthy of its title. The AEE lasted until 1880. In 1852, several players set up the United All-England Eleven as a rival to the AEE, and from 1857 to 1866 the annual match between these two teams was arguably the most important contest of the English season – certainly judged by the quality of the players.

- The 1873/4 team.

The early overseas tours were organised as purely commercial ventures, as indeed were the first Test-playing tours. The first such tour was to North America by a team of English professionals, departing England in September 1859. The team comprised six players from the All-England Eleven and six from the United All-England Eleven, and was captained by George Parr. They played five matches, winning them all. There were no first-class fixtures.

With the outbreak of the American Civil War, attention turned to Australia. The inaugural tour of the country took place in 1861–2, and was organised by Messrs Spiers & Pond. Led by HH Stephenson, the English team played 12 matches, but none were first-class.

In 1863–4, the Melbourne Cricket Club organised a tour by an English team under the captaincy of George Parr, which also visited New Zealand. The team played 16 matches, but none were first-class.

There were further tours of North America (taking in both the US and Canada) in late 1868, led by Edgar Willsher, and in late 1872, under R.A. Fitzgerald. The latter side included W.G.Grace.

In 1873–4, the Melbourne Cricket Club organised a tour by a team under the captaincy of WG Grace, which played 15 matches, but none were first-class.

Most of the matches of these early touring teams were played "against odds", that is to say the opposing team was permitted to have more than eleven players (usually twenty-two) in order to make a more even contest.

- 1877 to 1890

James Lillywhite, a professional with Sussex CCC, led a team which had sailed on the P&O steamship Poonah on 21 September 1876. They played in Australia and then New Zealand before returning to Australia to play a combined Australian XI, for once on even terms of XI a side. The match, starting on 15 March 1877 at the Melbourne Cricket Ground, came to be regarded as the first Test match, although none of its participants could have guessed at its significance at the time. Charles Bannerman, of Australia, faced the first ball and scored the first century, a glorious 165 before retiring hurt with a broken finger. The next highest score in this inaugural Test for Australia was Tom Horan with 10. Alfred Shaw of England bowled the first ball and took 5 for 38 in Australia's second innings. Tom Kendall, born in England, took 7 English wickets for 55 to bring Australia victory by 45 runs. 100 years later, in the Centenary Test, the result and margin would be exactly the same. England won a second match to square the series.

In 1878/79 Kent captain and MCC luminary Lord Harris took a team, consisting mainly of amateurs, to Australia where they lost by 10 wickets at Melbourne. Their batting was reasonably strong but the lack of professional bowlers cost them dear. The tour became famous for an unseemly incident in a tour game at Sydney where a near riot broke out. One of the umpires was Edmund Barton, who became Australia's first prime minister.

The 1880 Australian tourists were the first to play a Test match on English soil. Their 'demon' bowler, Fred Spofforth, sustained a hand injury and, crucially, missed the game in which W.G. Grace scored 152 and Billy Murdoch one run better. Lord Harris led the victorious England side at the Oval.

An all professional side, organised by Shaw, Shrewsbury and Lillywhite sailed to Australia for the 1881/82 campaign. The tour was bedeviled with scandal and allegations of fisticuffs, betting and heavy drinking. Tom Garrett took 18 wickets in the three Tests played for Australia. Many of the tour matches were still against local '22's. Australia won the four Test series 2 – 0.

The developing rivalry took on a new turn in 1882, when England lost at home at The Oval in the solitary Test of the summer. Spofforth took 7 for 46 and 7 for 44 and Ted Peate, Yorkshire slow left armer who had taken 8 wickets, was out just 8 runs short of victory. Upset at this turn of events, The Sporting Times printed an obituary to English cricket: "In

Affectionate Remembrance of ENGLISH CRICKET, which died at the Oval on 29th AUGUST 1882, Deeply lamented by a large circle of sorrowing friends and acquaintances R.I.P. N.B. – The body will be cremated and the ashes taken to Australia."

When England toured Australia the following winter of 1882/83 and won 2–1, the England captain, the Hon. Ivo Bligh was presented with an urn that contained some ashes, which have variously been said to be of a bail, ball or even a woman's veil. And so The Ashes series was born. Yorkshire stalwart Billy Bates, who played all his 15 Tests on 5 tours to Australia, scored 55 and took 14 for 102 at Melbourne in the second Test, including the first Test hat-trick, to bring England the first innings victory in Test cricket. A.G. Steel made 135* at Sydney – although he did drop Bonner 4 times (out of 8 drops in total) as the giant Australian hitter scored 87.

England won 1–0 in the three Test series in 1884. Peate took 6 for 85 in Australia's first innings, and Ulyett 7 for 36, the second as England won by an innings Lord's where Steel made a wonderful 148 out of England's first innings of 379. Australia's captain Billy Murdoch scored the first Test double hundred at the Oval where Walter Read of England hit a century in 113 minutes after going in at number 10. All 11 Englishmen bowled in Australia's innings, including wicket keeper Lyttelton with underarm lobs.

England embarked on a long stretch of dominance. They won 14 and lost only 3 of the Tests played between 1884 and 1890. Billy Barnes hit 134 in the opening Adelaide Test of the five Test 1884/85 series while Johnny Briggs of Lancashire hit a two-hour ton at Melbourne in the second, where Australia fielded a completely new team of 11 different players after a dispute over gate money. Wilfred Flowers scored 56 and took 5 for 46 in the third Test at Sydney where Australia pulled back a game thanks to Bonner smashing a century in even time. England won the deciding fifth Test by an innings at Melbourne, Arthur Shrewsbury making 105*.

W. G. Grace scored 170 in the Oval Test of 1886, beating the individual Test innings record of 164 set by Arthur Shrewsbury in the previous match on an evil pitch at Lords. England won by an innings on the third day after Australia were bowled out for 68 and 149m with George Lohmann of Surrey taking 12 for 104. The Australian tourists, without Bannerman or Murdoch and often losing Spofforth to injuries, lost all three Tests.

Shrewsbury's England beat Australia in both matches on the 1886–87 tour, despite being bowled out for 45 on the first day at Sydney. Two England parties toured there in 1887–88, with Shaw and Shrewsbury's team sponsored by Melbourne CC and Lord Harris's team by the Sydney Association. The two sides joined up for one Test Match at Sydney which they won thanks to Lohmann's 9 wickets and Bobby Peel's 10. Australia made just 42 and 82 on a poor pitch in bad light.

The 1888 Australians won at Lords but lost at The Oval and Old Trafford. Their bowling was penetrative, particularly Jack Ferris and the 'terror' Charlie Turner, but their batting was too weak to withstand the English professionals in their home conditions. Bobby Peel took 11 wickets at Old Trafford.

England won the first Test in South Africa, at Port Elizabeth in March 1889 by 8 wickets, despite fielding a less than first choice XI. W.H. Ashley took 7 for 95 for South Africa in his only Test. Bobby Abel of Surrey scored 120 for England in the Second Test, the first hundred scored in South Africa. Bernard Tancred of South Africa became the first Test batsman to carry his bat, for 26*, as South Africa collapsed to 47 all out. M.P. Bowden remains the youngest man to captain England, at just 23 years and 144 days. Johnny Briggs took 7 for 17 and 8 for 11 at Cape Town, 14 bowled and 1 LBW.

- 1890s

Four ball overs gave way to five ball overs in the 1890s and to six ball overs in Australia, as the game continued to develop quickly. England won the 1890 Ashes series 2–0, although Jack Barrett carried his bat for 67 through Australia's second innings of 176 at Lord's. W. G. Grace was out second ball in the first innings but saw England home in the second with 75*. Frederick Martin took 12 Australian wickets for 102 but 'Nutty' never played an Ashes match again. The third scheduled match, at Old Trafford, was the first Test to be abandoned without a ball being bowled.

W. G. Grace's tourists lost 2–1 on the 1891–92 tour, Australia winning at Melbourne and Sydney, where Bannerman batted for seven and a half hours and scored only three boundaries and England's Bobby Abel carried his bat for 132. England claimed a consolation innings victory at Adelaide where Stoddard scored 134 and Peel 83 and Briggs took 6 wickets in each innings.

England won the only Test on the 1891/92 tour of South Africa at Cape Town, where Harry Wood, the Surrey wicket keeper made 134 not out and Ferris, who had earlier played for Australia, took 13 for 91. Billy Murdoch was another Australian turned Englishman on the tour.

- England regained the Ashes in 1893, with an innings win at The Oval and draws in the other two Tests. W. G. Grace and A.E. Stoddart made three consecutive century opening stands. William Gunn of Nottinghamshire scored his only Test hundred, 102*, at Old Trafford, while Arthur Shrewsbury scored 106 at Lord's. Future England great Ranjitsinhji was one of the unfortunate bowlers as Australia set a new record team score of 843 against 'Oxford and Cambridge Past and Present' in Portsmouth.

Andrew Stoddart led England to a thrilling 3–2 victory on the 1894–1895 Ashes tour. Bobby Peel took the final wickets in the first Test victory at Sydney and the second at Melbourne and hit the winning runs in the final and deciding Test at the MCG. England's amazing victory at Sydney, by 10 runs, came after they had followed on with Lancashire's Albert Ward hitting 75 and 117 in the game. J.T. Brown scored 140 for England at Melbourne where England were set 297 to win. He reached 50 in 28 minutes and put on a then record 210 with Ward as England won by six wickets. Tom Richardson took 32 wickets in the Tests.

- England won all three Tests of the 1895/96 tour of South Africa by resounding margins. Lohmann was unplayable, taking 7 for 38 and 8 for 7 at Port Elizabeth and finishing with a hat trick. He took 9 for 28 and 3 for 43 at Johannesburg and 7 for 42 and 1 for 45 at Cape Town.

Having been overlooked for the first Test at Lord's, where Australian captain Harry Trott scored 143 and put on a record 210 with Syd Gregory (103), Shri Ranjitsinhji burst into Test cricket with 62 and 154 at Old Trafford in 1896. His magical batting and Tom Richardson's 13 for 244 were not enough to prevent Australia running out winners by 3 wickets however. Five English professionals went on 'strike' for more money before the Oval Test. Abel, Hayward and Richardson relented, but Gunn and Lohmann never played for England again. England won the series 2–1.

The Ashes were lost on Andrew Stoddart's 1897/98 tour, with Australia thumping England 4–1. Australian Joe Darling was the first batsmen to make 500 runs in a Test series, including 101 at Sydney, 178 at Adelaide and 160 in the final Sydney Test, where his hundred came up in 91 minutes. Stoddart's mother died just before the first Test and he was too distraught to play in either of the first two matches. Ranji, batting at number 7 after a throat infection, scored a brilliant 175 in the first Test and took England over 500 for the first time in a game won by 9 wickets but the Englishmen lost the next four heavily.

Lord Hawke's tourists in 1898/99 played and won two Tests in South Africa, with sometime Australian Albert Trott taking 17 wickets. Plum Warner carried his bat for 132 at Johannesburg in his maiden Test.

The 1899 series against Australia saw two significant developments. For the first time in England, five Tests were played rather than three, with Trent Bridge and Headingley being added to the "traditional" venues of Lord's, The Oval and Old Trafford. Also MCC and the counties appointed a selection committee for the first time. It comprised three active players: Lord Hawke, W.G. Grace and H.W. Bainbridge who was the captain of Warwickshire. Prior to this, England teams for home Tests had been chosen by the club on whose ground the match was to be played. The peerless Australian Victor Trumper dominated the series. He scored 1,500 runs on the tour, including 300 not out against Sussex and a breathtaking century in Australia's sole, but deciding, Test victory at Lords. W.G. Grace played his last Test at Trent Bridge. F.S. Jackson and Tom Hayward put on 185 at the Oval for the first wicket. England, scoring 576, forced Australia (352) to follow on, but the Australians played out the draw and with it retained the Ashes.

- 1900–1914: The "Golden Age"

The first Test series of the new century took place in Australia 1901–1902 and was won by Australia who came from one down to take the series 4–1. The England side was a private venture of Archie MacLaren (although the matches were all official Test matches). It was rather an attritional series of matches with only three centuries being scored and only one team innings over 400 (the first innings of England in the First Test at the SCG). Sydney Barnes made his debut for England and took 19 wickets in the first two Tests before being injured in the third and talking no further part in the series.

There was a home series against Australia in 1902 which was won by the Australians (2–1). In the drawn First Test at Edgbaston Australia were dismissed for 36 in their first innings (Wilfred Rhodes 7 for 17) but rain meant that the match was drawn. Rain also ruined the following match at Lord's. Sydney Barnes returned to the England team and had immediate success, taking seven wickets in the third Test at Sheffield (the only Test ever to be played there).

However England still lost the match. The final two Tests were amongst the most exciting of all time. A brilliant century by Trumper helped Australia to win the match at Old Trafford by three runs. England's batting throughout the series was modest with only one innings of over 300 and with only three centuries scored. The last of these was a match-winning innings in the final Test at The Oval by Gilbert Jessop, who went in at number seven in the second innings with England 48–5 and scored what was then the fastest century in Test cricket in 70 minutes, setting up an improbable England win by one wicket. The last wicket pair of Wilfred Rhodes and George Hirst nervelessly acquired the final fifteen runs needed for victory.

England toured Australia in 1903–1904, the first time that the MCC had been responsible for an England tour overseas. England regained The Ashes with a 3–2 series win under the captaincy of Plum Warner. In the first Test R.E.Foster made his Test debut and scored 287 in his first ever innings – the then highest ever Test score and a record that was to stand for a quarter of a century. Wilfred Rhodes took 15 wickets in England's second Test win at the MCG –a record that was to stand for thirty years. In the fifth Test England were dismissed for 61 in their first innings on a rain-affected pitch.

In 1905 Australia toured England and were beaten 2–0 with three matches drawn. Notable batting performances in the series included centuries by A.C. MacLaren, F.S. Jackson (2), Johnny Tyldesley (2) and C.B. Fry. B.J.T. Bosanquet, the inventor of the googly, took eight wickets in an Innings in the First Test.

In 1905–06 Plum Warner took an MCC team to South Africa for the first time and England were soundly beaten 4–1 in the series. England's batting faltered throughout the series with only one team innings in excess of 200 (successive innings of 184,190,148,160,295,196,198,160,187 and 130) and just one individual century (by F.L.Fane in the 3rd Test at the Wanderers). England's only win came at Newlands where the left-arm slow bowler Colin Blythe took eleven wickets in the match.

In 1907 there was a home three match Test series against South Africa which England, captained by R.E.Foster, won 1–0. Highlights included another sparkling innings by Gilbert Jessop who scored 93 at Lord's in a partnership of 145 for the sixth wicket with Len Braund who scored a century. There was another fine bowling performance by Blythe, who took 15 wickets at Headingley on a rain-affected match in a match that England won despite having been bowled out for 76 in their first innings.

In England's Test series in Australia in 1907–08 Australia won the first Test but England hit back well with a narrow win at the MCG in the 2nd Test in which Jack Hobbs made his England debut scoring 83 and 28. England were outplayed by Australia in the next three Tests and lost the series and the Ashes 4–1. England's batting was fragile throughout the series with only Gunn (2) and Hutchings scoring hundreds. The bowling relied on Jack Crawford), Arthur Fielder and Barnes, who took 79 wickets between them.

In a home series against Australia in 1909 England lost 2–1 (two draws) and no combination of players (England used 25 in total in the series) seemed to work. England failed to make 200 in an innings five times and there was only one individual century (by J. Sharp in the 3rd Test). The remarkable Colin Blythe delivered England's only victory by taking eleven wickets in the First Test at Edgbaston, but thereafter Australia, whilst never dominating the England attack, always had the edge.

England returned to South Africa in 1909–10 under H.D.G. Leveson-Gower, for a five match Test series and fared little better than on their first visit in 1905–06. The series was lost 3–2 but this disguises South Africa's superiority. The main highlight was Jack Hobbs first (of 15) Test century in the final Test at Newlands, he put on a then record 211 for the first wicket with Wilfred Rhodes. This was one of only two personal hundreds by England batsmen in the series. The bowling attack was weak – although the last of the great "lob" (underhand) bowlers George Simpson-Hayward had field days in the first three Test matches when he took a total of 21 wickets. Colin Blythe bowled England to a consolation win in the fifth Test with ten wickets in the match. Legspin dominated on the matting pitches, with the ball often bouncing chest high. Vogler took 29 wickets for the home side and Faulkner 29.

England toured Australia in 1911/12 under Plum Warner, but Johnny Douglas took over the captaincy when Warner fell ill prior to the first Test. Despite losing that first match at Sydney, a side which boasted Jack Hobbs, Frank Woolley, Sydney Barnes and Wilfred Rhodes hit back to take the next four Tests in style. Frank Foster and Barnes dominated with the ball, sharing 66 wickets, while Hobbs, Rhodes and Woolley recorded centuries. Hobbs and Rhodes shared opening stands of 147 at Adelaide and a then record 323 at Melbourne in the next Test where Barnes dismissed Bardsley, Kelleway, Hill and Armstrong for 3 runs in his opening spell. Later in the game, when the crowd barracked Barnes for deliberating over a field setting, he threw the ball down in disgust and refused to continue until order was restored. Frank Woolley also hit 305* in 205 minutes in a tour game against Tasmania.

The 1912 home season saw a unique experiment with a 9 Test triangular tournament involving South Africa and Australia but it was an idea ahead of its time and was not repeated. C.B. Fry of Sussex captained the team against Syd Gregory of Australia and Frank Mitchell of South Africa. Jack Hobbs scored 107 against Australia at Lords in a rain ruined game. The Australia v South Africa match, at Lord's, was notable for a visit by King George V, the first time a reigning monarch had watched Test cricket. Barnes took 34 wickets in his 3 Tests against the South Africans.

England's 1913/14 tour of South Africa was the last before the onset of World War I, and England dominated the rubber, winning 4–0. Syd Barnes was once again unplayable, taking 49 wickets in four Tests before boycotting the last in a row over his wife's accommodation. Only Herbie Taylor resisted for the home side, with skilful backfoot defence on the matting pitches, scoring 508 runs at 50.8.

- 1920s

England resumed their Test cricket after World War I with a tour of Australia in 1920/21 under Johnny Douglas. After the ravages of the war it was little surprise when England went down to a series of crushing defeats, the first 5–0 whitewash. Six Australians scored hundreds while Mailey spun out 36 English batsmen. Things were no better when Warwick Armstrong's men toured England in 1921. Australian fast bowlers Gregory and McDonald battered the English batsmen with a succession of bouncers and Jack Hobbs missed most of the season with first a leg injury then appendicitis. England used 30 players in all. Only one Australian made a century as opposed to 3 for England – A. C. "Jack" Russell scoring 101 and 102* and Phil Mead 182* – but Australia's 3–0 victory made it 8 Ashes defeats in succession.

England resumed the winning habit on the 1922/23 tour of South Africa, under F.T. Mann, winning a pulsating rubber 2 – 1. England lost the first Test but scraped to victory in the next, at Cape Town, by one wicket. Phil Mead scored 181 at Kingsmead, Durban, to ensure a draw and they won the fifth and final match, also at Durban, thanks to Jack Russell's twin centuries in his final Test. This dominance was underlined in England in 1924 with a 3–0 for England.

Hopes that the Ashes might be regained were dashed on the 1924/25 tour down under however, Australia thrashing England 4–1, although England scored 8 centuries to Australia's 6. Herbert Sutcliffe scored 734 runs at 81.56 and Maurice Tate broke Mailey's Ashes record with 38 wickets, bowling 2,528 balls in the Tests. England's only victory came at Melbourne, by an innings, after Captain Arthur Gilligan won the toss for the only time. It was England's first Ashes Test win in 12 years.

England drew the first four Tests of the 1926 Ashes series and so the series rested on the Oval Test, for which Percy Chapman replaced Arthur Carr as captain and both the 48-year-old Rhodes and 21-year-old Larwood were selected. Hobbs and Sutcliffe scored centuries and Australia lost by 289 runs. The South African team proved stronger than before however and drew the 1927/28 series 2–2.

A fourth team was, at last, introduced to Test cricket when the West Indies took their bow in 1928. England won each of the three Tests by an innings, Freeman taking 22 wickets, and a view was expressed in the press that their elevation had proved a mistake although 'electric heels' Learie Constantine did the double on the tour. The England team at this period was as strong as it has ever been and Australia were dispatched 4–1 on the 1928/29 Ashes tour. Hammond scored 44, 28, 251, 200, 32, 119*, 177, 38 and 16 – a total of 905 runs, a new record. Percy Chapman captained the team but barely played again.

England, under J. C. White and Arthur Carr, beat South Africa 2–0 at home in 1929 with Herbert Sutcliffe scoring a hundred in each innings at the Oval Bizarrely there were two concurrent England tours in 1929/30, one to New Zealand and one to the West Indies. Surrey paceman Maurice Allom took four wickets in five balls in New Zealand's maiden Test match, including a hat trick, and his 8 for 65 swept England to victory in Christchurch by 8 wickets with the three later Tests drawn. At the same time another England team were drawing 1–1 in the West Indies under F. S. G. Calthorpe. Forty-year-old Patsy Hendren made 1,765 runs on this tour and Andy Sandham scored 325 at Kingston (out of England's 849) in his final Test. The 'black Bradman' George Headley followed twin centuries at Georgetown with 223 in the same Kingston game.

- 1930s

The 21-year-old Don Bradman dominated the 1930 Ashes series in England, scoring 974 runs in his seven Test innings. He scored 254 at Lord's, 334 at Headingley, when Chapman stuck to attacking fields all day, and 232 at the Oval. Australia regained the Ashes. Harold Larwood took only four wickets in the series although K. S. Duleepsinhji made 173 at Lord's on debut.

England played five Tests in South Africa on the 1930/31 tour. Chasing 240 to win the first Test at the Old Wanderers ground in Johannesburg they were bowled out by E. P. Nupen, a master on the matting wicket, and drew the next four.

New Zealand played their first Test in England in 1931 and their strong performance at Lord's led the authorities to arrange another two that summer, one of which England won. India played their first Test in England in 1932 at Lords, reducing England to 19 for 3 on the first morning before losing a competitive match when they were bowled out for 187 chasing 346.

Bill Woodfull evades a Bodyline ball. Note the number of leg-side fielders.

Before the 1932–3 tour to Australia, England had become used to the prolific run-scoring of Don Bradman. The England captain, Surrey's Douglas Jardine chose to develop the already existing leg theory into fast leg theory, or bodyline, as a tactic to stop Bradman. Fast leg theory involved bowling fast balls directly at the batsman's body, and Jardine had two very fast accurate bowlers, Harold Larwood and Bill Voce to bowl them. The batsman would need to defend himself, and if he touched the ball with the bat, he risked being caught by one of a large number of fielders placed on the leg side.

England won the series and the Ashes 4–1. But complaints about the Bodyline tactic caused crowd disruption on the tour, and threats of diplomatic action from the Australian Cricket Board, which during the tour sent the following cable to the Marylebone Cricket Club in London:

Bodyline bowling assumed such proportions as to menace best interests of game, making protection of body by batsmen the main consideration. Causing intensely bitter feeling between players as well as injury. In our opinion is unsportsmanlike. Unless stopped at once likely to upset friendly relations existing between Australia and England.

Later, Jardine was removed from the captaincy and the laws of cricket changed so that no more than one fast ball aimed at the body was permitted per over, and having more than two fielders behind square leg were banned.

England won two Tests on the 1933/34 tour of India, the first ever Tests held in the sub continent. England won by nine wickets at Bombay's Gymkhana ground with Bryan Valentine scoring 136 in his first Test innings. Morris Nichols and E. W. "Nobby" Clark bowled so many bouncers at the Indian batsman that they wore solar topees instead of caps to protect themselves from the ball as much as the sun. Naoomal Jeoomal top edged a Clark bouncer into his head in the third Test, was unable to continue and didn't bat in the second innings.

Australia won the first Test of the 1934 Ashes series by 238 runs at Trent Bridge. Clarrie Grimmett took 25 wickets in the series, and Bill O'Reilly 28 as England were spun to defeat. Bradman made 758 runs in the Tests and 2020 on the tour, with Stan McCabe making 2078. Patsy Hendren(132) and Maurice Leyland (153) ensured a draw at Old Trafford and England did manage a rare Test win over Australia at Lord's with Hedley Verity taking 14 wickets in a day and 15 in the match. Bradman (304) and Ponsford (181) put on 388 at Headingley and then 451 at the Oval where England lost by a massive 562 runs. Ponsford scored 266 in his last Test. Nobby Clark bowled some 'leg theory' against the Australians, with little success. Bill Voce took 8 for 66 for Notts against the Australians but withdrew from the attack with a 'leg injury' after Woodfall raised discrete objections.

England toured the West Indies in 1934/5 and showed the folly of sending a weakened team as they lost the rubber 2–1 with George Headley scoring 270 not out in the 4th Test at Sabina Park. South Africa won on English soil for the first time, taking the 5 Test series 1–0 in 1935 with a victory at Lord's by 157 runs thanks to Bruce Mitchell's 164 and Jock Cameron's quickfire 90. Cameron died at 30, of enteric fever, soon after returning home from this tour.

India used 22 players in three Tests in England in 1936. A then record 588 runs were scored on the second day of the Old Trafford Test and England too experimented with their team and took the rubber 2–0.

The 1936/37 Ashes tour, under Gubby Allen, was a titanic struggle. England, helped by rain freshening the pitch, won by 322 runs in Brisbane and an innings in Sydney where Wally Hammond scored 271 not out. Bill Voce was their spearhead, taking 17 wickets in these two games. Bradman added a record 346 for the sixth wicket with Jack Fingleton at Melbourne and followed that with 212 at Adelaide where his team leveled the score at 2–2. Bradman, McCabe and Badcock all scored hundreds in the decider at Melbourne and Australian took the series 3–2.

England beat New Zealand 1–0 in a three Test rubber in 1937. Tom Goddard took 6 for 29 in bowling out the visitors for 134 at the Old Trafford Test as they chased 265 to win. Jack Cowie had taken 6 for 67 for New Zealand and 10 in the match. Len Hutton scored a century after having begun his England career with 0 and 1 at Lords. Prospective tours of South Africa and West Indies fell through in the winter of 1937/38.

The 1938 Ashes series was a high scoring affair. Hutton, Barnett, Paynter (216*) and Compton made hundreds at Trent Bridge with the Australians scoring three including Stan McCabe's brilliant 232.

Hammond scored 240 in the Lord's Test while Bill Brown made a double ton and Bradman a match saving century for Australia. Old Trafford fell victim to the rain and Australia retained the Ashes with a win at Headingley, thanks to Bradman's century and 10 wickets for O'Reilly and 7 for Fleetwood-Smith. England won the final Test at the Oval thanks to a record Test score of 903 – 7 dec and Len Hutton's world record of 364 in 13 hours, 17 minutes. Bradman, whose score of 334 had been surpassed, was the first to congratulate the 22-year-old Yorkshireman. Maurice Leyland made 187 and the elegant Joe Hardstaff 169 not out. Australia subsided to 201 and 123, batting 2 short, and England won by an innings and 579.

Paul Gibb scored 93 and 106 on debut at Johannesburg on England's 1938/39 tour. England scored 11 centuries in the series and South Africa 6. Paynter scored 117 and 100 in the first Test and 243 in the third at Durban. England, 1–0, in the series, returned to Durban to play a deciding 'timeless' Test to the finish. It was abandoned as a draw after 10 days as England had to catch the train to catch the boat home. Needing 696 to win they were, incredibly, 654 for 5, Gibb having scored 120, Hammond 140 and Edrich 219. A record 1981 runs were scored, and the concept of timeless Tests was abandoned.

The three Tests between England and the West Indies in 1939 were the last before the Second World War, although a team for an MCC tour of India was selected more in hope than expectation of the matches being played. Len Hutton and Denis Compton, leaders of the bright new batting generation, scored hundreds at Lords where the brilliant George Headley scored a ton in each innings. Hammond became the first fielder to hold 100 Test catches at Old Trafford. England took the series 1–0 as the war clouds loomed over Europe.

CHAPTER FOUR

History of cricket

- History of cricket

The sport of cricket has a known history beginning in the late 16th century. Having originated in south-east England, it became an established sport in the country in the 18th century and developed globally in the 19th and 20th centuries. International matches have been played since the 19th-century and formal Test cricket matches are considered to date from 1877. Cricket is the world's second most popular spectator sport after association football (soccer).

Internationally, cricket is governed by the International Cricket Council (ICC) which has over one hundred countries and territories in membership although only twelve currently play Test cricket.

- Origin

Cricket was probably created during Saxon or Norman times by children living in the Weald, an area of dense woodlands and clearings in south-east England that lies across Kent and Sussex. The first definite written reference is from the end of the 16th-century.

There have been several speculations about the game's origins, including some that it was created in France or Flanders. The earliest of these speculative references is from 1300 and concerns the future King Edward II playing at "creag and other games" in both Westminster and Newenden. It has been suggested that "creag" was an Old English word for cricket, but expert opinion is that it was an early spelling of "craic", meaning "fun and games in general".

It is generally believed that cricket survived as a children's game for many generations before it was increasingly taken up by adults around the beginning of the 17th century. Possibly cricket was derived from bowls, assuming bowls is the older sport, by the intervention of a batsman trying to stop the ball from reaching its target by hitting it away. Playing on sheep-grazed land or in clearings, the original implements may have been a matted lump of sheep's wool (or even a stone or a small lump of wood) as the ball; a stick or a crook or another farm tool as the bat; and a stool or a tree stump or a gate (e.g., a wicket gate) as the wicket.

- First definite reference

John Derrick was a pupil at the Royal Grammar School, then the Free School, in Guildford when he and his friends played creckett circa 1550

In 1597 (Old Style – 1598 New Style) a court case in England concerning an ownership dispute over a plot of common land in Guildford, Surrey, mentions the game of creckett. A 59-year-old coroner, John Derrick, testified that he and his school friends had played creckett on the site fifty years earlier when they attended the Free School. Derrick's account proves beyond reasonable doubt that the game was being played in Surrey circa 1550, and is the earliest universally accepted reference to the game.

The first reference to cricket being played as an adult sport was in 1611, when two men in Sussex were prosecuted for playing cricket on Sunday instead of going to church. In the same year, a dictionary defined cricket as a boys' game, and this suggests that adult participation was a recent development.

- Derivation of the name of "cricket"

A number of words are thought to be possible sources for the term "cricket". In the earliest definite reference, it was spelled creckett. The name may have been derived from the Middle Dutch krick(-e), meaning a stick; or the Old English cricc or cryce meaning a crutch or staff, or the French word criquet meaning a wooden post. The Middle Dutch word krickstoel means a long low stool used for kneeling in church; this resembled the long low wicket with two stumps used in early cricket. According to Heiner Gillmeister, a European language expert of the University of Bonn, "cricket" derives from the Middle Dutch phrase for hockey, met de (krik ket)sen (i.e., "with the stick chase").

It is more likely that the terminology of cricket was based on words in use in south-east England at the time and, given trade connections with the County of Flanders, especially in the 15th century when it belonged to the Duchy of Burgundy, many Middle Dutch words found their way into southern English dialects.

- The Commonwealth

After the Civil War ended in 1648, the new Puritan government clamped down on "unlawful assemblies", in particular the more raucous sports such as football. Their laws also demanded a stricter observance of the Sabbath than there had been previously. As the Sabbath was the only free time available to the lower classes, cricket's popularity may have waned during the Commonwealth. However, it did flourish in public fee-paying schools such as Winchester and St Paul's. There is no actual evidence that Oliver Cromwell's regime banned cricket specifically and there are references to it during the interregnum that suggest it was acceptable to the authorities provided that it did not cause any "breach of the Sabbath". It is believed that the nobility in general adopted cricket at this time through involvement in village games.

- Gambling and press coverage

Cricket thrived after the Restoration in 1660 and is believed to have first attracted gamblers making large bets at this time. It is possible, as believed by some historians, that top-class matches began. In 1664, the "Cavalier" Parliament passed the Gaming Act 1664 which limited stakes to £100, although that was still a fortune at the time, equivalent to about £16,000 in present-day terms. Cricket had become a significant gambling sport by the end of the 17th century, as evidenced in 1697 by a newspaper report of a "great match" played in Sussex which was 11-a-side and played for high stakes of 50 guineas a side.

With freedom of the press having been granted in 1696, cricket for the first time could be reported in the newspapers. But it was a long time before the newspaper industry adapted sufficiently to provide frequent, let alone comprehensive, coverage of the game. During the first half of the 18th century, press reports tended to focus on the betting rather than on the play.

- 18th-century cricket

Gambling introduced the first patrons because some of the gamblers decided to strengthen their bets by forming their own teams and it is believed the first "county teams" were formed in the aftermath of the Restoration in 1660, especially as members of the nobility were employing "local experts" from village cricket as the earliest professionals. The first known game in which the teams use county names is in 1709 but there can be little doubt that these sort of fixtures were being arranged long before that. The match in 1697 was probably Sussex versus another county.

The most notable of the early patrons were a group of aristocrats and businessmen who were active from about 1725, which is the time that press coverage became more regular, perhaps as a result of the patrons' influence. These men included the 2nd Duke of Richmond, Sir William Gage, Alan Brodrick and Edwin Stead. For the first time, the press mentions individual players like Thomas Waymark.

- Cricket expands beyond England

Cricket was introduced to North America via the English colonies in the 17th century, probably before it had even reached the north of England. In the 18th century it arrived in other parts of the globe. It was introduced to the West Indies by colonists and to India by East India Company mariners in the first half of the century. It arrived in Australia almost as soon as colonisation began in 1788. New Zealand and South Africa followed in the early years of the 19th century.

Cricket never caught on in Canada, despite efforts by the upper class to promote the game as a way of identifying with the "mother country". Canada, unlike Australia and the West Indies, witnessed a continual decline in the popularity of the game during 1860 to 1960. Linked in the public consciousness to an upper-class sport, the game never became popular with the general public. In the summer season it had to compete with baseball. During the First World War, Canadian units stationed in France played baseball instead of cricket.

- Development Laws of Cricket

It's not clear when the basic rules of cricket such as bat and ball, the wicket, pitch dimensions, overs, how out, etc. were originally formulated. In 1728, the Duke of Richmond and Alan Brodick drew up Articles of Agreement to determine the code of practice in a particular game and this became a common feature, especially around payment of stake money and distributing the winnings given the importance of gambling.

In 1744, the Laws of Cricket were codified for the first time and then amended in 1774, when innovations such as lbw, middle stump and maximum bat width were added. These laws stated that "the principals shall choose from amongst the gentlemen present two umpires who shall absolutely decide all disputes". The codes were drawn up by the so-called "Star and Garter Club" whose members ultimately founded the Marylebone Cricket Club at Lord's in 1787. The MCC immediately became the custodian of the Laws and has made periodic revisions and recodifications subsequently.

- Continued growth in England

The game continued to spread throughout England, and, in 1751, Yorkshire is first mentioned as a venue. The original form of bowling (i.e., rolling the ball along the ground as in bowls) was superseded sometime after 1760 when bowlers began to pitch the ball and study variations in line, length and pace. Scorecards began to be kept on a regular basis from 1772; since then, an increasingly clear picture has emerged of the sport's development.

- An artwork depicting the history of the cricket bat

The first famous clubs were London and Dartford in the early 18th century. London played its matches on the Artillery Ground, which still exists. Others followed, particularly Slindon in Sussex, which was backed by the Duke of Richmond and featured the star player Richard Newland. There were other prominent clubs at Maidenhead, Hornchurch, Maidstone, Sevenoaks, Bromley, Addington, Hadlow and Chertsey.

But far and away the most famous of the early clubs was Hambledon in Hampshire. It started as a parish organisation that first achieved prominence in 1756. The club itself was founded in the 1760s and was well patronised to the extent that it was the focal point of the game for about thirty years until the formation of MCC and the opening of Lord's Cricket Ground in 1787. Hambledon produced several outstanding players including the master batsman John Small and the first great fast bowler Thomas Brett. Their most notable opponent was the Chertsey and Surrey bowler Edward "Lumpy" Stevens, who is believed to have been the main proponent of the flighted delivery.

It was in answer to the flighted, or pitched, delivery that the straight bat was introduced. The old "hockey stick"–style of bat was only really effective against the ball being trundled or skimmed along the ground. First-class cricket began, retrospectively, in 1772.A Game of Cricket at The Royal Academy Club in Marylebone Fields, now Regent's Park, depiction by unknown artist, c. 1790–1799

- History of cricket (1772–1815) and History of English cricket (1816–1863)

The game also underwent a fundamental change of organisation with the formation for the first time of county clubs. All the modern county clubs, starting with Sussex in 1839, were founded during the 19th century. No sooner had the first county clubs established themselves than they faced what amounted to "player action" as William Clarke created the travelling All-England Eleven in 1846. Though a commercial venture, this team did much to popularise the game in districts which had never previously been visited by high-class cricketers. Other similar teams were created and this vogue lasted for about thirty years. But the counties and MCC prevailed.

- A cricket match at Darnall, Sheffield in the 1820s.

The growth of cricket in the mid and late 19th century was assisted by the development of the railway network. For the first time, teams from a long distance apart could play one other without a prohibitively time-consuming journey. Spectators could travel longer distances to matches, increasing the size of crowds. Army units around the Empire had time on their hands, and encouraged the locals so they could have some entertaining competition. Most of the Empire embraced cricket, with the exception of Canada.

In 1864, another bowling revolution resulted in the legalisation of overarm and in the same year. W. G. Grace began his long and influential career at this time, his feats doing much to increase cricket's popularity.

He introduced technical innovations which revolutionised the game, particularly in batting.

- International cricket begins

The first ever international cricket game was between the US and Canada in 1844. The match was played at the grounds of the St George's Cricket Club in New York.

- The English team 1859 on their way to the US

In 1859, a team of leading English professionals set off to North America on the first-ever overseas tour and, in 1862, the first English team toured Australia. Between May and October 1868, a team of Aboriginal Australians toured England in what was the first Australian cricket team to travel overseas.

- The first Australian touring team (1878) pictured at Niagara Falls

In 1877, an England touring team in Australia played two matches against full Australian XIs that are now regarded as the inaugural Test matches. The following year, the Australians toured England for the first time and the success of this tour ensured a popular demand for similar ventures in future. No Tests were played in 1878 but more soon followed and, at The Oval in 1882, the Australian victory in a tense finish gave rise to The Ashes.South Africa became the third Test nation in 1889.

- National championships

A significant development in domestic cricket occurred in 1890 when the official County Championship was constituted in England. Soon afterwards, in May 1894, the sport's first-class standard was officially defined. This organisational initiative has been repeated in other countries. Australia established the Sheffield Shield in 1892–93. Other national competitions to be established were the Currie Cup in South Africa, the Plunket Shield in New Zealand and the Ranji Trophy in India. The ICC re-defined first-class status in 1947 as a global concept.

The period from 1890 to the outbreak of the First World War has become one of nostalgia, ostensibly because the teams played cricket according to "the spirit of the game", but more realistically because it was a peacetime period that was shattered by the First World War. The era has been called The Golden Age of cricket and it featured numerous great names such as Grace, Wilfred Rhodes, C. B. Fry, Ranjitsinhji and Victor Trumper.

- Balls per over

During most of the 19th-century standard overs were made up of four deliveries. In 1889 five-ball overs were introduced in first-class cricket, with a move to generally use six-ball overs in 1900.

In the 20th-century, eight-ball overs were used at times in a number of countries, primarily Australia, where eight-balls were the standard over length between 1918/19 and 1978/79, South Africa and New Zealand. Since the 1979/80 Australian and New Zealand seasons, six balls per over have been used worldwide, and the most recent version of the Laws only permits six-ball overs.

- Growth of international cricket

Sid Barnes traps Lala Amarnath lbw in the first official Test between Australia and India at the MCG in 1948

The Imperial Cricket Conference was founded in 1909 with England, Australia and South Africa as the founder members. This aimed to regulate international cricket between the three sides, considered the only three of equal status at the time. West Indies were admitted as members in 1928, allowing them to play Test cricket against the other sides. New Zealand and India both became Test playing nations before World War II and Pakistan joined soon afterwards in 1952.

At the initial suggestion of Pakistan, the ICC was expanded to include non-Test playing countries from 1965, with Associate members being admitted. At the same time the organisation changed its name to the International Cricket Conference. The first limited-overs World Cups were played during the 1970s and Sri Lanka became the first Associate member to be raised to Test playing status in 1982.

The international game continued to grow with the introduction of Affiliate Member status in 1984, a level of membership designed for sides with less history of playing cricket. In 1989 the ICC renamed itself the International Cricket Council. Zimbabwe became Full Members in 1992 and Bangladesh in 2000 before Afghanistan and Ireland were both admitted as Test sides in 2018, bringing the number of full members of the ICC to 12.

- International cricket in South Africa from 1971 to 1981

The greatest crisis to hit international cricket was brought about by apartheid, the South African policy of racial segregation. The situation began to crystallise after 1961 when South Africa left the Commonwealth of Nations and so, under the rules of the day, its cricket board had to leave the International Cricket Conference (ICC). Cricket's opposition to apartheid intensified in 1968 with the cancellation of England's tour to South Africa by the South African authorities, due to the inclusion in the England team of Basil D'Oliveira, a Cape Coloured player. In 1970, the ICC members voted to suspend South Africa indefinitely from international cricket competition.

Starved of top-level competition for its best players, the South African Cricket Board began funding so-called "rebel tours", offering large sums of money for international players to form teams and tour South Africa. The ICC's response was to blacklist any rebel players who agreed to tour South Africa, banning them from officially sanctioned international cricket. As players were poorly remunerated during the 1970s, several accepted the offer to tour South Africa, particularly players getting towards the end of their careers for which a blacklisting would have little effect.

The rebel tours continued into the 1980s but then progress was made in South African politics and it became clear that apartheid was ending. South Africa, now a "Rainbow Nation" under Nelson Mandela, was welcomed back into international sport in 1991.

- World Series Cricket

The money problems of top cricketers were also the root cause of another cricketing crisis that arose in 1977 when the Australian media magnate Kerry Packer fell out with the Australian Cricket Board over TV rights. Taking advantage of the low remuneration paid to players, Packer retaliated by signing several of the best players in the world to a privately run cricket league outside the structure of international cricket. World Series Cricket hired some of the banned South African players and allowed them to show off their skills in an international arena against other world-class players. The schism lasted only until 1979 and the "rebel" players were allowed back into established international cricket, though many found that their national teams had moved on without them. Long-term results of World Series Cricket have included the introduction of significantly higher player salaries and innovations such as coloured kit and night games.

- Limited-overs cricket

In the 1960s, English county teams began playing a version of cricket with games of only one innings each and a maximum number of overs per innings. Starting in 1963 as a knockout competition only, limited-overs cricket grew in popularity and, in 1969, a national league was created which consequently caused a reduction in the number of matches in the County Championship. The status of limited overs matches is governed by the official List A categorisation. Although many "traditional" cricket fans objected to the shorter form of the game, limited-overs cricket did have the advantage of delivering a result to spectators within a single day; it did improve cricket's appeal to younger or busier people; and it did prove commercially successful.

The first limited-overs international match took place at Melbourne Cricket Ground in 1971 as a time-filler after a Test match had been abandoned because of heavy rain on the opening days. It was tried simply as an experiment and to give the players some exercise, but turned out to be immensely popular. limited-overs internationals (LOIs or ODIs—one-day internationals) have since grown to become a massively popular form of the game, especially for busy people who want to be able to see a whole match. The International Cricket Council reacted to this development by organising the first Cricket World Cup in England in 1975, with all the Test-playing nations taking part.

- Analytic and graphic technology

Limited-overs cricket increased television ratings for cricket coverage. Innovative techniques introduced in coverage of limited-over matches were soon adopted for Test coverage. The innovations included presentation of in-depth statistics and graphical analysis, placing miniature cameras in the stumps, multiple usage of cameras to provide shots from several locations around the ground, high-speed photography and computer graphics technology enabling television viewers to study the course of a delivery and help them understand an umpire's decision.

In 1992, the use of a third umpire to adjudicate run-out appeals with television replays was introduced in the Test series between South Africa and India. The third umpire's duties have subsequently expanded to include decisions on other aspects of play such as stumpings, catches and boundaries. From 2011, the third umpire was being called upon to moderate review of umpires' decisions, including lbw, with the aid of virtual-reality tracking technologies (e.g., Hawk-Eye and Hot Spot), though such measures still could not free some disputed decisions from heated controversy.

- 21st-century cricket

In June 2001, the ICC introduced a "Test Championship Table" and, in October 2002, a "One-day International Championship Table". As indicated by ICC rankings, the various cricket formats have continued to be a major competitive sport in most former British Empire countries, notably the Indian subcontinent, and new participants including the Netherlands. In 2017, the number of countries with full ICC membership was increased to twelve by the addition of Afghanistan and Ireland.

The ICC expanded its development programme, aiming to produce more national teams capable of competing at the various formats. Development efforts are focused on African and Asian nations, and on the United States. In 2004, the ICC Intercontinental Cup brought first-class cricket to 12 nations, mostly for the first time. Cricket's newest innovation is Twenty20, essentially an evening entertainment. It has so far enjoyed enormous popularity and has attracted large attendances at matches as well as good TV audience ratings. The inaugural ICC Twenty20 World Cup tournament was held in 2007. The formation of Twenty20 leagues in India – the unofficial Indian Cricket League, which started in 2007, and the official Indian Premier League, starting in 2008 – raised much speculation in the cricketing press about their effect on the future of cricket.

CHAPTER FIVE

What Is Cricket ?

- What Is Cricket ?

Cricket is a bat-and-ball game played between two teams of eleven players on a field at the centre of which is a 22-yard (20-metre) pitch with a wicket at each end, each comprising two bails balanced on three stumps. The game proceeds when a player on the fielding team, called the bowler, "bowls" (propels) the ball from one end of the pitch towards the wicket at the other end. The batting side's players score runs by striking the bowled ball with a bat and running between the wickets, while the bowling side tries to prevent this by keeping the ball within the field and getting it to either wicket, and dismiss each batter (so they are "out"). Means of dismissal include being bowled, when the ball hits the stumps and dislodges the bails, and by the fielding side either catching a hit ball before it touches the ground, or hitting a wicket with the ball before a batter can cross the crease line in front of the wicket to complete a run. When ten batters have been dismissed, the innings ends and the teams swap roles. The game is adjudicated by two umpires, aided by a third umpire and match referee in international matches.

Forms of cricket range from Twenty20, with each team batting for a single innings of 20 overs and the game generally lasting three hours, to Test matches played over five days. Traditionally cricketers play in all-white kit, but in limited overs cricket they wear club or team colours. In addition to the basic kit, some players wear protective gear to prevent injury caused by the ball, which is a hard, solid spheroid made of compressed leather with a slightly raised sewn seam enclosing a cork core layered with tightly wound string.

The earliest reference to cricket is in South East England in the mid-16th century. It spread globally with the expansion of the British Empire, with the first international matches in the second half of the 19th century. The game's governing body is the International Cricket Council (ICC), which has over 100 members, twelve of which are full members who play Test matches. The game's rules, the Laws of Cricket, are maintained by Marylebone Cricket Club (MCC) in London. The sport is followed primarily in South Asia, Australasia, the United Kingdom, southern Africa and the West Indies.Women's cricket, which is organised and played separately, has also achieved international standard. The most successful side playing international cricket is Australia, which has won seven One Day International trophies, including five World Cups, more than any other country and has been the top-rated Test side more than any other country.

- History of cricket to 1725

A medieval "club ball" game involving an underhand bowl towards a batter. Ball catchers are shown positioning themselves to catch a ball. Detail from the Canticles of Holy Mary, 13th century.

Cricket is one of many games in the "club ball" sphere that basically involve hitting a ball with a hand-held implement; others include baseball (which shares many similarities with cricket, both belonging in the more specific bat-and-ball games category), golf, hockey, tennis, squash, badminton and table tennis. In cricket's case, a key difference is the existence of a solid target structure, the wicket (originally, it is thought, a "wicket gate" through which sheep were herded), that the batter must defend. The cricket historian Harry Altham identified three "groups" of "club ball" games: the "hockey group", in which the ball is driven to and fro between two targets (the goals); the "golf group", in which the ball is driven towards an undefended target (the hole); and the "cricket group", in which "the ball is aimed at a mark (the wicket) and driven away from it".

It is generally believed that cricket originated as a children's game in the south-eastern counties of England, sometime during the medieval period.Although there are claims for prior dates, the earliest definite reference to cricket being played comes from evidence given at a court case in Guildford in January 1597 (Old Style), equating to January 1598 in the modern calendar. The case concerned ownership of a certain plot of land and the court heard the testimony of a 59-year-old coroner, John Derrick, who gave witness that.

Being a scholler in the ffree schoole of Guldeford hee and diverse of his fellows did runne and play there at creckett and other plaies.

Given Derrick's age, it was about half a century earlier when he was at school and so it is certain that cricket was being played c. 1550 by boys in Surrey. The view that it was originally a children's game is reinforced by Randle Cotgrave's 1611 English-French dictionary in which he defined the noun "crosse" as "the crooked staff wherewith boys play at cricket" and the verb form "crosser" as "to play at cricket".

One possible source for the sport's name is the Old English word "cryce" (or "cricc") meaning a crutch or staff. In Samuel Johnson's Dictionary, he derived cricket from "cryce, Saxon, a stick". In Old French, the word "criquet" seems to have meant a kind of club or stick. Given the strong medieval trade connections between south-east England and the County of Flanders when the latter belonged to the Duchy of Burgundy, the name may have been derived from the Middle Dutch (in use in Flanders at the time) "krick"(-e), meaning a stick (crook). Another possible source is the Middle Dutch word "krickstoel", meaning a long low stool used for kneeling in church and which resembled the long low wicket with two stumps used in early cricket. According to Heiner Gillmeister, a European language expert of Bonn University, "cricket" derives from the Middle Dutch phrase for hockey, met de (krik ket)sen (i.e., "with the stick chase"). Gillmeister has suggested that not only the name but also the sport itself may be of Flemish origin.

- Growth of amateur and professional cricket in England

Evolution of the cricket bat. The original "hockey stick" (left) evolved into the straight bat from c. 1760 when pitched delivery bowling began.

Although the main object of the game has always been to score the most runs, the early form of cricket differed from the modern game in certain key technical aspects; the North American variant of cricket known as wicket retained many of these aspects. The ball was bowled underarm by the bowler and along the ground towards a batter armed with a bat that in shape resembled a hockey stick; the batter defended a low, two-stump wicket; and runs were called notches because the scorers recorded them by notching tally sticks.

In 1611, the year Cotgrave's dictionary was published, ecclesiastical court records at Sidlesham in Sussex state that two parishioners, Bartholomew Wyatt and Richard Latter, failed to attend church on Easter Sunday because they were playing cricket. They were fined 12d each and ordered to do penance.This is the earliest mention of adult participation in cricket and it was around the same time that the earliest known organised inter-parish or village match was played – at Chevening, Kent. In 1624, a player called Jasper Vinall died after he was accidentally struck on the head during a match between two parish teams in Sussex.

Cricket remained a low-key local pursuit for much of the 17th century. It is known, through numerous references found in the records of ecclesiastical court cases, to have been proscribed at times by the Puritans before and during the Commonwealth. The problem was nearly always the issue of Sunday play as the Puritans considered cricket to be "profane" if played on the Sabbath, especially if large crowds or gambling were involved.

According to the social historian Derek Birley, there was a "great upsurge of sport after the Restoration" in 1660. Gambling on sport became a problem significant enough for Parliament to pass the 1664 Gambling Act, limiting stakes to £100 which was, in any case, a colossal sum exceeding the annual income of 99% of the population. Along with prizefighting, horse racing and blood sports, cricket was perceived to be a gambling sport.Rich patrons made matches for high stakes, forming teams in which they engaged the first professional players.By the end of the century, cricket had developed into a major sport that was spreading throughout England and was already being taken abroad by English mariners and colonisers – the earliest reference to cricket overseas is dated 1676. A 1697 newspaper report survives of "a great cricket match" played in Sussex "for fifty guineas apiece" – this is the earliest known contest that is generally considered a First Class match.

- The patrons, and other players from the social class known as the "gentry", began to classify themselves as "amateurs" to establish a clear distinction from the professionals, who were invariably members of the working class, even to the point of having separate changing and dining facilities. The gentry, including such high-ranking nobles as the Dukes of Richmond, exerted their honour code of noblesse oblige to claim rights of leadership in any sporting contests they took part in, especially as it was necessary for them to play alongside their "social inferiors" if they were to win their bets. In time, a perception took hold that the typical amateur who played in first-class cricket, until 1962 when amateurism was abolished, was someone with a public school education who had then gone to one of Cambridge or Oxford University – society insisted that such people were "officers and gentlemen" whose destiny was to provide leadership. In a purely financial sense, the cricketing amateur would theoretically claim expenses for playing while his professional counterpart played under contract and was paid a wage or match fee; in practice, many amateurs claimed more than actual expenditure and the derisive term "shamateur" was coined to describe the practice.

- The Young Cricketer, 1768

The game underwent major development in the 18th century to become England's national sport.Its success was underwritten by the twin necessities of patronage and betting. Cricket was prominent in London as early as 1707 and, in the middle years of the century, large crowds flocked to matches on the Artillery Ground in Finsbury. The single wicket form of the sport attracted huge crowds and wagers to match, its popularity peaking in the 1748 season. Bowling underwent an evolution around 1760 when bowlers began to pitch the ball instead of rolling or skimming it towards the batter. This caused a revolution in bat design because, to deal with the bouncing ball, it was necessary to introduce the modern straight bat in place of the old "hockey stick" shape.

The Hambledon Club was founded in the 1760s and, for the next twenty years until the formation of Marylebone Cricket Club (MCC) and the opening of Lord's Old Ground in 1787, Hambledon was both the game's greatest club and its focal point. MCC quickly became the sport's premier club and the custodian of the Laws of Cricket. New Laws introduced in the latter part of the 18th century included the three stump wicket and leg before wicket (lbw).

The 19th century saw underarm bowling superseded by first roundarm and then overarm bowling. Both developments were controversial.Organisation of the game at county level led to the creation of the county clubs, starting with Sussex in 1839. In December 1889, the eight leading county clubs formed the official County Championship, which began in 1890.

The most famous player of the 19th century was W. G. Grace, who started his long and influential career in 1865. It was especially during the career of Grace that the distinction between amateurs and professionals became blurred by the existence of players like him who were nominally amateur but, in terms of their financial gain, de facto professional. Grace himself was said to have been paid more money for playing cricket than any professional.

The last two decades before the First World War have been called the "Golden Age of cricket". It is a nostalgic name prompted by the collective sense of loss resulting from the war, but the period did produce some great players and memorable matches, especially as organised competition at county and Test level developed.

- Cricket becomes an international sport

In 1844, the first-ever international match took place between the United States and Canada. In 1859, a team of English players went to North America on the first overseas tour. Meanwhile, the British Empire had been instrumental in spreading the game overseas and by the middle of the 19th century it had become well established in Australia, the Caribbean, India, Pakistan, New Zealand, North America and South Africa.

In 1862, an English team made the first tour of Australia. The first Australian team to travel overseas consisted of Aboriginal stockmen who toured England in 1868. The first One Day International match was played on 5 January 1971 between Australia and England at the Melbourne Cricket Ground.

In 1876–77, an England team took part in what was retrospectively recognised as the first-ever Test match at the Melbourne Cricket Ground against Australia. The rivalry between England and Australia gave birth to The Ashes in 1882, and this has remained Test cricket's most famous contest. Test cricket began to expand in 1888–89 when South Africa played England.

- World cricket in the 20th century

The inter-war years were dominated by Australia's Don Bradman, statistically the greatest Test batter of all time. Test cricket continued to expand during the 20th century with the addition of the West Indies (1928),

New Zealand (1930) and India (1932) before the Second World War and then Pakistan (1952), Sri Lanka (1982), Zimbabwe (1992), Bangladesh (2000), Ireland and Afghanistan (both 2018) in the post-war period. South Africa was banned from international cricket from 1970 to 1992 as part of the apartheid boycott.

- The rise of limited overs cricket

Cricket entered a new era in 1963 when English counties introduced the limited overs variant. As it was sure to produce a result, limited overs cricket was lucrative and the number of matches increased. The first Limited Overs International was played in 1971 and the governing International Cricket Council (ICC), seeing its potential, staged the first limited overs Cricket World Cup in 1975. In the 21st century, a new limited overs form, Twenty20, made an immediate impact. On 22 June 2017, Afghanistan and Ireland became the 11th and 12th ICC full members, enabling them to play Test cricket.

- A typical cricket field.

In cricket, the rules of the game are specified in a code called The Laws of Cricket (hereinafter called "the Laws") which has a global remit. There are 42 Laws (always written with a capital "L"). The earliest known version of the code was drafted in 1744 and, since 1788, it has been owned and maintained by its custodian, the Marylebone Cricket Club (MCC) in London.

- Playing area

Cricket is a bat-and-ball game played on a cricket field between two teams of eleven players each. The field is usually circular or oval in shape and the edge of the playing area is marked by a boundary, which may be a fence, part of the stands, a rope, a painted line or a combination of these; the boundary must if possible be marked along its entire length.

In the approximate centre of the field is a rectangular pitch (see image, below) on which a wooden target called a wicket is sited at each end; the wickets are placed 22 yards (20 m) apart. The pitch is a flat surface 10 feet (3.0 m) wide, with very short grass that tends to be worn away as the game progresses (cricket can also be played on artificial surfaces, notably matting). Each wicket is made of three wooden stumps topped by two bails.

- Cricket pitch and creases

As illustrated above, the pitch is marked at each end with four white painted lines: a bowling crease, a popping crease and two return creases. The three stumps are aligned centrally on the bowling crease, which is eight feet eight inches long. The popping crease is drawn four feet in front of the bowling crease and parallel to it; although it is drawn as a twelve-foot line (six feet either side of the wicket), it is, in fact, unlimited in length. The return creases are drawn at right angles to the popping crease so that they intersect the ends of the bowling crease; each return crease is drawn as an eight-foot line, so that it extends four feet behind the bowling crease, but is also, in fact, unlimited in length.

Before a match begins, the team captains (who are also players) toss a coin to decide which team will bat first and so take the first innings. Innings is the term used for each phase of play in the match.In each innings, one team bats, attempting to score runs, while the other team bowls and fields the ball, attempting to restrict the scoring and dismiss the batters. When the first innings ends, the teams change roles; there can be two to four innings depending upon the type of match. A match with four scheduled innings is played over three to five days; a match with two scheduled innings is usually completed in a single day. During an innings, all eleven members of the fielding team take the field, but usually only two members of the batting team are on the field at any given time. The exception to this is if a batter has any type of illness or injury restricting his or her ability to run, in this case the batter is allowed a runner who can run between the wickets when the batter hits a scoring run or runs,though this does not apply in international cricket. The order of batters is usually announced just before the match, but it can be varied.

The main objective of each team is to score more runs than their opponents but, in some forms of cricket, it is also necessary to dismiss all of the opposition batters in their final innings in order to win the match, which would otherwise be drawn. If the team batting last is all out having scored fewer runs than their opponents, they are said to have "lost by n runs" (where n is the difference between the aggregate number of runs scored by the teams). If the team that bats last scores enough runs to win, it is said to have "won by n wickets", where n is the number of wickets left to fall. For example, a team that passes its opponents‘ total having lost six wickets (i.e., six of their batters have been dismissed) have won the match "by four wickets".

In a two-innings-a-side match, one team's combined first and second innings total may be less than the other side's first innings total. The team with the greater score is then said to have "won by an innings and n runs", and does not need to bat again: n is the difference between the two teams' aggregate scores. If the team batting last is all out, and both sides have scored the same number of runs, then the match is a tie; this result is quite rare in matches of two innings a side with only 62 happening in first-class matches from the earliest known instance in 1741 until January 2017. In the traditional form of the game, if the time allotted for the match expires before either side can win, then the game is declared a draw.

If the match has only a single innings per side, then a maximum number of overs applies to each innings. Such a match is called a "limited overs" or "one-day" match, and the side scoring more runs wins regardless of the number of wickets lost, so that a draw cannot occur. In some cases, ties are broken by having each team bat for a one-over innings known as a Super Over; subsequent Super Overs may be played if the first Super Over ends in a tie. If this kind of match is temporarily interrupted by bad weather, then a complex mathematical formula, known as the Duckworth–Lewis–Stern method after its developers, is often used to recalculate a new target score. A one-day match can also be declared a "no-result" if fewer than a previously agreed number of overs have been bowled by either team, in circumstances that make normal resumption of play impossible; for example, wet weather.

In all forms of cricket, the umpires can abandon the match if bad light or rain makes it impossible to continue. There have been instances of entire matches, even Test matches scheduled to be played over five days, being lost to bad weather without a ball being bowled: for example, the third Test of the 1970/71 series in Australia.

- Innings

The innings (ending with 's' in both singular and plural form) is the term used for each phase of play during a match. Depending on the type of match being played, each team has either one or two innings. Sometimes all eleven members of the batting side take a turn to bat but, for various reasons, an innings can end before they have all done so. The innings terminates if the batting team is "all out", a term defined by the Laws: "at the fall of a wicket or the retirement of a batter, further balls remain to be bowled but no further batter is available to come in". In this situation, one of the batters has not been dismissed and is termed not out; this is because he has no partners left and there must always be two active batters while the innings is in progress.

- An innings may end early while there are still two not out batters

the batting team's captain may declare the innings closed even though some of his players have not had a turn to bat: this is a tactical decision by the captain, usually because he believes his team have scored sufficient runs and need time to dismiss the opposition in their innings

the set number of overs (i.e., in a limited overs match) have been bowled

the match has ended prematurely due to bad weather or running out of time

in the final innings of the match, the batting side has reached its target and won the game.

- Overs

The Laws state that, throughout an innings, "the ball shall be bowled from each end alternately in overs of 6 balls". The name "over" came about because the umpire calls "Over!" when six balls have been bowled. At this point, another bowler is deployed at the other end, and the fielding side changes ends while the batters do not. A bowler cannot bowl two successive overs, although a bowler can (and usually does) bowl alternate overs, from the same end, for several overs which are termed a "spell". The batters do not change ends at the end of the over, and so the one who was non-striker is now the striker and vice versa. The umpires also change positions so that the one who was at "square leg" now stands behind the wicket at the non-striker's end and vice versa.

- Clothing and equipment

English cricketer W. G. Grace "taking guard" in 1883. His pads and bat are very similar to those used today. The gloves have evolved somewhat. Many modern players use more defensive equipment than were available to Grace, most notably helmets and arm guards.

The wicket-keeper (a specialised fielder behind the batter) and the batters wear protective gear because of the hardness of the ball, which can be delivered at speeds of more than 145 kilometres per hour (90 mph) and presents a major health and safety concern. Protective clothing includes pads (designed to protect the knees and shins), batting gloves or wicket-keeper's gloves for the hands, a safety helmet for the head and a box for male players inside the trousers (to protect the crotch area). Some batters wear additional padding inside their shirts and trousers such as thigh pads, arm pads, rib protectors and shoulder pads. The only fielders allowed to wear protective gear are those in positions very close to the batter (i.e., if they are alongside or in front of him), but they cannot wear gloves or external leg guards.

Subject to certain variations, on-field clothing generally includes a collared shirt with short or long sleeves; long trousers; woolen pullover (if needed); cricket cap (for fielding) or a safety helmet; and spiked shoes or boots to increase traction. The kit is traditionally all white and this remains the case in Test and first-class cricket but, in limited overs cricket, team colours are worn instead.

- Bat and ball

Two types of cricket ball, both of the same size:

i) A used white ball. White balls are mainly used in limited overs cricket, especially in matches played at night, under floodlights (left).

ii) A used red ball. Red balls are used in Test cricket, first-class cricket and some other forms of cricket (right).

The essence of the sport is that a bowler delivers (i.e., bowls) the ball from his or her end of the pitch towards the batter who, armed with a bat, is "on strike" at the other end (see next sub-section: Basic gameplay).

The bat is made of wood, usually Salix alba (white willow), and has the shape of a blade topped by a cylindrical handle. The blade must not be more than 4.25 inches (10.8 cm) wide and the total length of the bat not more than 38 inches (97 cm). There is no standard for the weight, which is usually between 2 lb 7 oz and 3 lb (1.1 and 1.4 kg).

The ball is a hard leather-seamed spheroid, with a circumference of 9 inches (23 cm). The ball has a "seam": six rows of stitches attaching the leather shell of the ball to the string and cork interior. The seam on a new ball is prominent and helps the bowler propel it in a less predictable manner. During matches, the quality of the ball deteriorates to a point where it is no longer usable; during the course of this deterioration, its behaviour in flight will change and can influence the outcome of the match. Players will, therefore, attempt to modify the ball's behaviour by modifying its physical properties. Polishing the ball and wetting it with sweat or saliva is legal, even when the polishing is deliberately done on one side only to increase the ball's swing through the air, but the acts of rubbing other substances into the ball, scratching the surface or picking at the seam are illegal ball tampering.

- Player roles

Basic gameplay: bowler to batter

During normal play, thirteen players and two umpires are on the field. Two of the players are batters and the rest are all eleven members of the fielding team. The other nine players in the batting team are off the field in the pavilion. The image with overlay below shows what is happening when a ball is being bowled and which of the personnel are on or close to the pitch.

- Return crease

In the photo, the two batters (3 & 8; wearing yellow) have taken position at each end of the pitch (6). Three members of the fielding team (4, 10 & 11; wearing dark blue) are in shot. One of the two umpires (1; wearing white hat) is stationed behind the wicket (2) at the bowler's (4) end of the pitch. The bowler (4) is bowling the ball (5) from his end of the pitch to the batter at the other end who is called the "striker". The other batter (3) at the bowling end is called the "non-striker". The wicket-keeper (10), who is a specialist, is positioned behind the striker's wicket (9) and behind him stands one of the fielders in a position called "first slip" (11). While the bowler and the first slip are wearing conventional kit only, the two batters and the wicket-keeper are wearing protective gear including safety helmets, padded gloves and leg guards (pads).

While the umpire (1) in shot stands at the bowler's end of the pitch, his colleague stands in the outfield, usually in or near the fielding position called "square leg", so that he is in line with the popping crease (7) at the striker's end of the pitch. The bowling crease (not numbered) is the one on which the wicket is located between the return creases (12). The bowler (4) intends to hit the wicket (9) with the ball (5) or, at least, to prevent the striker (8) from scoring runs. The striker (8) intends, by using his bat, to defend his wicket and, if possible, to hit the ball away from the pitch in order to score runs.

Some players are skilled in both batting and bowling, or as either or these as well as wicket-keeping, so are termed all-rounders. Bowlers are classified according to their style, generally as fast bowlers, seam bowlers or spinners. Batters are classified according to whether they are right-handed or left-handed.

- Fielding

Of the eleven fielders, three are in shot in the image above. The other eight are elsewhere on the field, their positions determined on a tactical basis by the captain or the bowler. Fielders often change position between deliveries, again as directed by the captain or bowler.

If a fielder is injured or becomes ill during a match, a substitute is allowed to field instead of him, but the substitute cannot bowl or act as a captain, except in the case of concussion substitutes in international cricket. The substitute leaves the field when the injured player is fit to return. The Laws of Cricket were updated in 2017 to allow substitutes to act as wicket-keepers.

- Bowling and dismissal

Glenn McGrath of Australia holds the world record for most wickets in the Cricket World Cup.

Most bowlers are considered specialists in that they are selected for the team because of their skill as a bowler, although some are all-rounders and even specialist batters bowl occasionally. The specialists bowl several times during an innings but may not bowl two overs consecutively. If the captain wants a bowler to "change ends", another bowler must temporarily fill in so that the change is not immediate.

A bowler reaches his delivery stride by means of a "run-up" and an over is deemed to have begun when the bowler starts his run-up for the first delivery of that over, the ball then being "in play".

Fast bowlers, needing momentum, take a lengthy run up while bowlers with a slow delivery take no more than a couple of steps before bowling. The fastest bowlers can deliver the ball at a speed of over 145 kilometres per hour (90 mph) and they sometimes rely on sheer speed to try to defeat the batter, who is forced to react very quickly.

Other fast bowlers rely on a mixture of speed and guile by making the ball seam or swing (i.e. curve) in flight. This type of delivery can deceive a batter into miscuing his shot, for example, so that the ball just touches the edge of the bat and can then be "caught behind" by the wicket-keeper or a slip fielder. At the other end of the bowling scale is the spin bowler who bowls at a relatively slow pace and relies entirely on guile to deceive the batter. A spinner will often "buy his wicket" by "tossing one up" (in a slower, steeper parabolic path) to lure the batter into making a poor shot. The batter has to be very wary of such deliveries as they are often "flighted" or spun so that the ball will not behave quite as he expects and he could be "trapped" into getting himself out. In between the pacemen and the spinners are the medium paced seamers who rely on persistent accuracy to try to contain the rate of scoring and wear down the batter's concentration.

There are nine ways in which a batter can be dismissed: five relatively common and four extremely rare. The common forms of dismissal are bowled, caught, leg before wicket (lbw), run out and stumped. Rare methods are hit wicket,hit the ball twice, obstructing the field and timed out. The Laws state that the fielding team, usually the bowler in practice, must appeal for a dismissal before the umpire can give his decision. If the batter is out, the umpire raises a forefinger and says "Out!"; otherwise, he will shake his head and say "Not out".There is, effectively, a tenth method of dismissal, retired out, which is not an on-field dismissal as such but rather a retrospective one for which no fielder is credited.

- Batting, runs and extras

The directions in which a right-handed batter, facing down the page, intends to send the ball when playing various cricketing shots. The diagram for a left-handed batter is a mirror image of this one.

Batters take turns to bat via a batting order which is decided beforehand by the team captain and presented to the umpires, though the order remains flexible when the captain officially nominates the team. Substitute batters are generally not allowed, except in the case of concussion substitutes in international cricket.

In order to begin batting the batter first adopts a batting stance. Standardly, this involves adopting a slight crouch with the feet pointing across the front of the wicket, looking in the direction of the bowler, and holding the bat so it passes over the feet and so its tip can rest on the ground near to the toes of the back foot.

A skilled batter can use a wide array of "shots" or "strokes" in both defensive and attacking mode. The idea is to hit the ball to the best effect with the flat surface of the bat's blade. If the ball touches the side of the bat it is called an "edge". The batter does not have to play a shot and can allow the ball to go through to the wicketkeeper. Equally, he does not have to attempt a run when he hits the ball with his bat. Batters do not always seek to hit the ball as hard as possible, and a good player can score runs just by making a deft stroke with a turn of the wrists or by simply "blocking" the ball but directing it away from fielders so that he has time to take a run. A wide variety of shots are played, the batter's repertoire including strokes named according to the style of swing and the direction aimed: e.g., "cut", "drive", "hook", "pull".

The batter on strike (i.e. the "striker") must prevent the ball hitting the wicket, and try to score runs by hitting the ball with his bat so that he and his partner have time to run from one end of the pitch to the other before the fielding side can return the ball. To register a run, both runners must touch the ground behind the popping crease with either their bats or their bodies (the batters carry their bats as they run). Each completed run increments the score of both the team and the striker.

- Sachin Tendulkar is the only player to have scored one hundred international centuries

The decision to attempt a run is ideally made by the batter who has the better view of the ball's progress, and this is communicated by calling: usually "yes", "no" or "wait". More than one run can be scored from a single hit: hits worth one to three runs are common, but the size of the field is such that it is usually difficult to run four or more. To compensate for this, hits that reach the boundary of the field are automatically awarded four runs if the ball touches the ground en route to the boundary or six runs if the ball clears the boundary without touching the ground within the boundary. In these cases the batters do not need to run. Hits for five are unusual and generally rely on the help of "overthrows" by a fielder returning the ball. If an odd number of runs is scored by the striker, the two batters have changed ends, and the one who was non-striker is now the striker. Only the striker can score individual runs, but all runs are added to the team's total.

Additional runs can be gained by the batting team as extras (called "sundries" in Australia) due to errors made by the fielding side. This is achieved in four ways: no-ball, a penalty of one extra conceded by the bowler if he breaks the rules; wide, a penalty of one extra conceded by the bowler if he bowls so that the ball is out of the batter's reach bye, an extra awarded if the batter misses the ball and it goes past the wicket-keeper and gives the batters time to run in the conventional way leg bye, as for a bye except that the ball has hit the batter's body, though not his bat. If the bowler has conceded a no-ball or a wide, his team incurs an additional penalty because that ball (i.e., delivery) has to be bowled again and hence the batting side has the opportunity to score more runs from this extra ball.

- Specialist roles

Captain (cricket) and Wicket-keeper

The captain is often the most experienced player in the team, certainly the most tactically astute, and can possess any of the main skillsets as a batter, a bowler or a wicket-keeper. Within the Laws, the captain has certain responsibilities in terms of nominating his players to the umpires before the match and ensuring that his players conduct themselves "within the spirit and traditions of the game as well as within the Laws".

The wicket-keeper (sometimes called simply the "keeper") is a specialist fielder subject to various rules within the Laws about his equipment and demeanour. He is the only member of the fielding side who can effect a stumping and is the only one permitted to wear gloves and external leg guards. Depending on their primary skills, the other ten players in the team tend to be classified as specialist batters or specialist bowlers. Generally, a team will include five or six specialist batters and four or five specialist bowlers, plus the wicket-keeper.

- Umpires and scorers

The game on the field is regulated by the two umpires, one of whom stands behind the wicket at the bowler's end, the other in a position called "square leg" which is about 15–20 metres away from the batter on strike and in line with the popping crease on which he is taking guard. The umpires have several responsibilities including adjudication on whether a ball has been correctly bowled (i.e., not a no-ball or a wide); when a run is scored; whether a batter is out (the fielding side must first appeal to the umpire, usually with the phrase "How's that?" or "Owzat?"); when intervals start and end; and the suitability of the pitch, field and weather for playing the game. The umpires are authorised to interrupt or even abandon a match due to circumstances likely to endanger the players, such as a damp pitch or deterioration of the light.

Off the field in televised matches, there is usually a third umpire who can make decisions on certain incidents with the aid of video evidence. The third umpire is mandatory under the playing conditions for Test and Limited Overs International matches played between two ICC full member countries. These matches also have a match referee whose job is to ensure that play is within the Laws and the spirit of the game.

The match details, including runs and dismissals, are recorded by two official scorers, one representing each team. The scorers are directed by the hand signals of an umpire . For example, the umpire raises a forefinger to signal that the batter is out (has been dismissed); he raises both arms above his head if the batter has hit the ball for six runs. The scorers are required by the Laws to record all runs scored, wickets taken and overs bowled; in practice, they also note significant amounts of additional data relating to the game.

A match's statistics are summarised on a scorecard. Prior to the popularisation of scorecards, most scoring was done by men sitting on vantage points cuttings notches on tally sticks and runs were originally called notches.According to Rowland Bowen, the earliest known scorecard templates were introduced in 1776 by T. Pratt of Sevenoaks and soon came into general use.It is believed that scorecards were printed and sold at Lord's for the first time in 1846.

- thank you for buy & read this book

have a great day of your
from : Mr Vivek Kumar Pandey

- This All Credit Goes To My Super Hero Daddy. “Always Love You dad’.